The Art of Paisley

Ed Rossbach

VNR VAN NOSTRAND REINHOLD COMPANY
New York   Cincinnati   Toronto   London   Melbourne

Printed in the United States of America
Designed by Loudan Enterprises

Published by Van Nostrand Reinhold Company
A division of Litton Educational Publishing, Inc.
135 West 50th Street, New York, NY 10020, U.S.A.

Van Nostrand Reinhold Limited
1410 Birchmount Road
Scarborough, Ontario M1P 2E7, Canada

Van Nostrand Reinhold Australia Pty. Ltd.
17 Queen Street
Mitcham, Victoria 3132, Australia

Van Nostrand Reinhold Company Limited
Molly Millars Lane
Wokingham, Berkshire, England

16 15 14 13 12 11 10 9 8 7 6 5 4 3 2 1

Library of Congress Cataloging in Publication
Rossbach, Ed.
    The art of Paisley.
    Bibliography: p.
    Includes index.
    1. Shawls—Scotland—Paisley.   2. Textile fabrics—
Scotland—Paisley.   I. Title.
NK8945.P34R67   746.9'2   79-25587
ISBN 0-442-24346-4

Acknowledgments

Long before this project was completed it had become unusually burdensome. So many people had been generous in sharing information, directing me to material, lending me examples, and expressing an interest in the work, that I finally felt heavily obliged to produce a result almost as a token of my appreciation. More than I can say, I value the help of Reiko Mochinaga Brandon, Pat Charley, Marie Chesley, Peter Collingwood, Lia Cook, Lillian Elliott, Valerie England, Judy Fox, Donna Garaventa, Pat Hickman, Lisa Lee, Maureen Lochrie, Alice Marcoux, Mary Pettis, Maureen Irle Toftner, Katy Webb and Susan Wick. I am grateful for having been allowed to photograph at the Pioneer Museum, Victoria and Albert Museum, Cluny Museum, Robert H. Lowie Museum of Anthropology, and Paisley Museum and Art Galleries, and for having had access to the photo collections at the Metropolitan Museum of Art, Victoria and Albert Museum, Paisley Museum and Art Galleries, and the American Museum of Natural History. I greatly appreciate the beautiful photos given to me by the Musée de l'Impression sur Etoffes de Mulhouse. I am especially grateful for having been allowed to obtain a copy of the unpublished thesis of Brenda Gaskin. I appreciate the research support I received from the University of California, and the use of its collections in Berkeley, and its libraries in Berkeley and Davis.

I thank my wife for her somewhat wavering interest in the project over so many years. Because of Paisley, we made trips to Scotland that we would not otherwise have done since we are naturally attracted to southern climates. Forever mixed with my thoughts of Paisley shawls are Oban and Loch Lomond, the splendid greenhouse and the Central Hotel in Glasgow, and the Isle of Mull, where Dr. Johnson lost his walking stick—only a few years, it seems, before I started this Paisley project.

Contents

Foreword

Cashmere shawls became fashionable in Western Europe late in the eighteenth century. Because of the scarcity of material and slow manufacture, these handwoven textiles from India were very expensive.

Imitations were soon produced in Europe. Those from the town of Paisley, in Scotland, became world-famous as Paisley shawls.

Today the designation "Paisley shawl" often includes all Paisley-type shawls, regardless of where they were made. Even Cashmere shawls are often mistakenly called Paisleys. An entire shawl is a Paisley; the characteristic design motive is a Paisley; and patterns that use the Paisley motive are Paisley patterns, or Paisleys.

Introduction

In England, recently, I looked for old prints showing Paisley shawls being worn. The proprietress of a shop in Chester said, "They're lovely things, Paisleys. I have three. I don't wear them often—I don't have many occasions." Only a few weeks earlier, a curator had told me that his museum in San Francisco stopped accepting Paisley shawls because the textile collection was getting lopsided. I was astonished to discover that, although these shawls have not been woven for 100 years, they continue to be abundant and familiar.

Unlike many other textiles left from the past, Paisleys were not saved in church treasuries or preserved in desert burials. Instead, like coverlets and patchwork quilts, they were put away in family chests and trunks as the valued possessions of common people who cherished them beyond all others. Ordinary people were pleased to own garments such as even the Queen of England was said to have worn.

During the nineteenth century, these shawls were worn prominently at all festal occasions, as well as to church and market. They were identified in a ceremonial way with birth, marriage, and death. Women received shawls as wedding gifts from their betrothed—the shawls were described as the universal bridal present; brides were kirked in them, that is, the shawls were worn to church the first Sunday after marriage; babies were christened in the shawls; mothers wore the shawl to church as part of the purification following the birth of a child; a grandmother could say, "I have just ae wish when I'm laid awa, an' that is, that I'll be rolled in my Paisley an' laid beside my Donald."[1]

Paisley shawls were far more than a fashion; they were ceremonial garments with a significance understood throughout society. While other old garments were discarded, Paisleys were saved, sometimes even though threadbare, with the good parts patched and reassembled. A shawl was identified with its owner throughout her entire adult life. Finally, a shawl was part of a family and like a photograph in an album or a written message—perhaps with greater intensity—recalled the woman who once owned it.

To a remarkable extent, Paisley shawls were like folk textiles, such as the dowry embroideries from the Greek Islands, made for specific purposes and used in age-old rituals. Except, of course, the Paisleys were not peasant textiles, and they were not made by the women who wore them. While this distinction would seem to be momentous, the identification between a shawl and its owner was pretty much the same as between an embroidery and its maker. The personal feeling—the sense of identity—inspired by the traditional homemade textile was somehow transferred to the store-bought Paisley.

To visit the Pioneer Museum in Salt Lake City is to experience Paisley shawls. Here the memorabilia of the nineteenth century pioneers are collected and exhibited. Other museums display only selected items, the best of each kind; the Pioneer Museum displays everything, grouped according to family or camp. The saved things are arranged in the most straightforward and unpretentious manner, with the textiles neatly folded and stacked. Nothing is anonymous. Everything relates to people named and shown in compelling photographs. A label on each shawl tells who owned it, who gave it to her, where she brought it from and the year. To see the shawls the viewer must look also at the other cherished belongings of each family; nothing can be viewed apart from its surroundings. The quantity of shawls, each showing only a folded edge of pattern and color, is unforgettable. Someone in the museum explained the preponderance of shawls among the saved things; they were one touch of elegance that pioneer women had, and the women clung to these in spite of all hardships.

Today, when people—even those who know nothing about textiles—come across Paisleys that have been in the family for years, they recognize them as special, to be treated with respect. The size of these textiles, their full, heavy color and density of pattern, their fringes, make them seem substantial and important. While the shawls inevitably speak of their time, they speak also of something earlier, more distant. People describe them uncertainly as Persian or Indian. The Victorianism is mingled with the foreign. The shawls seem confusingly exotic, just as they did when they were new.

While their abundance today is directly related to their massive production, it is also directly related to their quality as textiles and to the special regard in which these textiles were held by their original owners and by each generation whose hands they passed through.

The deep human response to Paisleys is seldom reflected in the various writings about shawls. Other aspects are emphasized because the years of the shawl industry coincided with the years known as the Textile Phase of the industrial revolution. During the critical period of changeover from handweaving to powerweaving in Britain, the method of producing Paisleys was constantly changing in response to new conditions. Paisleys are often classified as examples of the new machine textiles and are deplored for being different from the splendid handwoven shawls from India. Actually, Paisleys are transitional textiles, belonging to the world of the handmade that was dying and the world of the machine-made that was being born. Although the shawls reflect the mechanical invention and innovation—and indeed the commercialism—of those years, the Paisleys relate just as clearly to the handlooms and the handcraft skills that preceded the revolution.

Shawl manufacture was like an old-fashioned novel with a beginning, a middle and an ending. Everything happened within a relatively short time. Early in the nineteenth century shawls began to be woven in Paisley; in about 1820 the manufacture of the shawls that are known today as Paisleys was in full swing; between 1840 and 1870 the trade was at its peak; about 1870 the shawl went out of fashion; between 1870 and 1880 the manufacture declined dramatically; in 1886 the last such shawl was woven in Paisley.

What took centuries in other textile expressions—Gothic tapestries, Greek Island embroideries, Coptic weavings, English ecclesiastical embroideries—happened quickly and decisively with Paisleys. The appearance, flowering and decay occurred within a person's life span. Because ancient and new processes alike were replaced with such rapidity, everything seemed alive and challenging, and modern. Shawl manufacture ended with such finality that those who had participated in it were able to look back on what they had known as though surveying the life of someone who had died.

Today, although the shawl production occurred such a relatively short time ago, enormous gaps exist in what is known about the shawls and their manufacture. As with textiles much more ancient than Paisley shawls, the objects remain as the best or only evidence. Paisley shawls have become historical textiles; they are a document, difficult to decipher, of ingenious technical solutions to problems of textile construction at a time when technological change was transforming the world.

The Paisley shawl is especially tantalizing among textiles since so much was known so recently and since so much is *almost* known today. For one reason or another, makers of other great textiles left textiles but no recollections of their experience or their responses to them. But Paisley textile workers, who had a reputation for their literacy and thoughtfulness, were conscious of their role in textile history. In their old age, several Paisley weavers looked back nostalgically and published their recollections. These works are the most tantalizing of all; they *almost* tell. An early photographer left several photographs of weavers standing outside their door; so many other photographs might have been taken. Drawings could have been made of the equipment; working designs could have been saved; examples could have been preserved; experiences could have been recollected, documented. Literate people had the information such a short time ago.

Today, the response to Paisley shawls is mixed. They are often categorized as Victorian design when much Victorian decorative art is dismissed as bad taste. To some people, the shawls (once they have been determined to be Paisleys rather than the prestigious Cashmeres) inspire a predictable stereotype response: Paisleys are mass-produced, machine-made copies of the beautiful handmade Cashmere shawls; since the machine is degrading to aesthetic quality and since sheer quantity is in itself aesthetically degrading, Paisleys are regrettable, inferior. Shawls have been described as "the first piece of clothing to fall victim to the corruption of taste that mass production encouraged."[2]

Fortunately, Paisleys can be evaluated without reliance upon a book authority—the kind of reliance that is necessary when only a few examples remain and when conditions of fading and decomposition prohibit anyone but an expert from assessing the original quality. Many Paisley shawls are in mint condition, the colors fresh, the fibers flexible and lively, and the structure unimpaired. They are not isolated in museum cases but can be touched, manipulated, lived with. Paisley shawls occasionally appear made up into clothing, or upholstery, or as decorative table covers and piano throws, and, of course, as wall hangings. Pieces of Paisley shawls have even been preserved, beaded and made into evening bags. In the model of a Georgian room at the city museum in Chester, England, Chippendale-type mahogany chairs are up-holstered in Paisley-type textiles; while in the Victorian model two shawls are prominent, one as a table cover and the other as a throw over a settee. Early in the shawl industry, the distinctive patterns and textures became familiar as more than shawls. Printed and woven textiles with the shawl designs were manufactured especially for upholstery and clothing fabric. Paisley patterns in innumerable variations for men's silk neckties and dressing robes, and women's dress fabrics, as well as for upholstery and kitchen plastic, have kept the shawls themselves familiar, easy to identify with. One way or another, Paisley shawls have continued to be experienced as textiles.

Many years before I became interested in Paisley shawls, I read a publication of the Victoria and Albert Museum in London saying that certain fabrics that satisfied the needs and tastes of a particular time in history "have at later periods been regarded as singularly happy combinations of sound work-manship, pleasing texture, and beautiful design."[3] Examples were Coptic tapestries, English ecclesiastical embroideries, Persian carpets, and French and Italian silks. When I recalled the statement years later, I unintentionally trans-formed it into something less happy, pleasing, sound and beautiful (I was greatly surprised when I reread the original statement). What I remembered was: now and then the essential character—the dynamics—of a society has been expressed by fiber. The ingenuity, energy, inventiveness and aesthetic sensitivity of the society went into the fiber arts to produce a group of textiles unlike all others, and immediately recognizable wherever they appear. Paisleys belong with this group.

To me, Paisley shawls are the final and brilliant expression of European craft handweaving. When the great tradition of European hand-weaving was dying, master weavers displayed their technical virtuosity in lively competition, vying with each other and also with the handweavers of India, Persia, and Turkey. And for a while they were vying with the new mechanisms that were certain to replace them. More than skills were chal-lenged. Pushing the complex handloom mechanism to its maximum potential became a lively exercise. Everything was innovation and invention and exuber-ance. The result was a miraculous outpouring of textiles, often of surpassing beauty and always of dazzling technical complexity. What an appropriate and moving swan song.

1. The Shawls
How they became fashionable

Although Paisley shawls were still being woven 100 years ago, the industry was on the decline, suffering hard times. It had suffered before and revived, but this time nothing would save it—no change in fashion, no public encouragement from Queen Victoria, no lowering of weavers' wages to reduce costs.

Many people had lived their lives without knowing a time when fancy shawls from the Scottish town of Paisley were not fashionable. Since their introduction early in the nineteenth century, Paisley shawls had figured prominently in the fashion scene and had adapted successfully to the most extreme changes in clothing style without losing their usefulness or their identity as distinctive and beautiful textiles. Why should they not continue to be useful and popular forever?

Europe, with its constructed clothing, its careful assembly of pieces to mold the fashionable figure, and its remarkably rapid changes in styles, had resorted to the shawl for comfortable protection. A convenient garment, it went over everything.

The demand for shawls started in the eighteenth century with the

(Left) Detail, Spitalfields silk, about 1736. This brocade is typical of the painterly florals, open and airy against generous backgrounds, that were popular in the eighteenth century. (Collection: Victoria & Albert Museum)

(Right) Detail, twill-tapestry Cashmere shawl. Although the pattern is floral, the flowers, leaves and stems are conventionalized and forced into an arbitrary outer shape. The jagged outlines are characteristic of the twill-tapestry technique. When Cashmeres were imitated by Europeans, angular contours and severe formal repetition of motives gave way to extravagant curves and dense compositions that often incorporated the naturalistic flower forms that Europeans loved. (Collection: Program in Visual Design, University of California, Berkeley)

appearance in Europe of exceptionally rare and beautiful textiles from Asia. Among these were Cashmere shawls, noble garments woven from the fleece of the Central Asian mountain goat and worn by men in India as shoulder mantles. The shawls were soft in texture and refined in workmanship and design—and of great beauty. Their reception in Europe can only be imagined: how both men and women were attracted to these luxurious textiles; how people handled them and experimented with them, trying them on in various ways, across the shoulders, across one shoulder, over the head, tied as a sash. In Proust's great novel, *The Remembrance of Things Past,* he describes the father wearing a white nightshirt crowned with a pink and violet Cashmere shawl tied around his head because he suffered from neuralgia. By the late eighteenth century, the shawls had become well-known articles of women's dress in England, admired for their warmth and lightness rather than for their patterns and colors.

France was the fashion center of Europe. When Cashmeres appeared there somewhat later than in England (they were described as an English fashion), Empire styles were reacting against a long period of formal clothing. The silks of Lyon, which had been fashionable for so many years, were often stiff taffetas and brocades. Little difference existed between silk for costumes and silk for furniture upholstery. Change came when fine cotton fabrics were brought from India in the middle of the eighteenth century. These textiles were light, diaphanous. New styles required not the stiff silks and wools but lightweight cloth with soft drape and flowing lines. The Cashmere shawls were at first not treated as fashionable garments but as a sort of yardage of appealing texture to be cut up and made into other clothing such as petticoats. Shawls became popular as outer garments when they proved to be warmer than silk, while showing the female figure to advantage. French women of wealth and position discarded their stiff wool and silk cloaks in favor of the new garment. Soon shawls were the rage, fashionable throughout Western Europe.

The Cashmere patterns were not what Europeans were accustomed to. For years, designs in European woven silk and printed cotton had been naturalistic florals, charmingly graceful, with pretty patterns casually and informally distributed. These woven silks were accomplished on complex looms that miraculously produced effects as free as the painted sketches of the artists. By contrast, the Cashmere patterns were woven on simple looms; they were formal and ordered, with regular spacing. Although floral and sometimes described as semi-naturalistic, they were not the naturalistic flower patterns of European textiles. The Cashmeres had a simple angularity, forthrightly expressing the horizontal-vertical nature of woven structure.

Without any humility the Europeans, in about 1850, started to demand improvements in the Cashmere designs to bring them up to European taste standards. Painted designs were sent to India from Europe to be woven as Cashmere shawls. At the same time, Indian designers borrowed motives from French design books and English wallpaper samples, often not comprehending the meaning of what they were copying. European designers, in turn, imitated and modified these until any clear identity was lost—where the motives came from originally, exactly what they were meant to be. The practice continued for years, with designs being expressed in various textile mediums—weaving, printing, embroidering, patchwork—under widely varied circumstances, with very different equipment and materials. The resulting amalgam of Asian and European motives was accepted by the public as pleasantly strange, romantic, and, of course, authentic. Fashion contrived to enjoy the best of both worlds: exotic foreign goods that exactly conformed to European taste.

The new shawls, with their sinuous draping, invited graceful ways of moving, standing, sitting, reclining. The shawls gave idle women something to do with their hands. Because women had to be specially practiced in dealing with the new garment, professional instruction was offered in the draping of a shawl. Ladies were described as "well-draped" rather than well-dressed.

Just as Queen Victoria was later to be identified with the Paisley shawls, Empress Josephine was identified with Cashmeres, albeit in a somewhat different way. Both noble ladies were controlling forces in the fashion scene, and both owned many shawls in which they appeared publicly. Victoria's public association with Paisleys became a hard-nosed gesture to bolster the faltering economy of Scotland. Josephine's pure fondness for the luxurious Cashmeres characterized the world of French fashion. She was an early participant in the shawl scene, when Cashmere shawls could be treated like other cloth on the market, to be cut up and reassembled. She had Cashmere shawls converted into gowns, bedquilts and even cushions for her dog. In addition, she had hundreds of Cashmeres that she wore as shawls. (Napoleon is described yanking a Cashmere from Josephine's shoulders and tossing it into the fire, since he preferred seeing her shoulders exposed.)

To touch a fine old Cashmere shawl today is to marvel at its waxen smoothness and glossiness, so unlike silk, although it is described as silken. To let such a shawl move through the hands is to experience the sensuous pleasure that so recommended the shawls to self-indulgent women of fashion.

An appreciation of the Cashmere shawls for their unique quality as woven fiber rather than for their patterns and colors is not to be underestimated, no matter how surprising it may seem today. A piece of woven Cashmere, free of dyed color and patterning, offers a glorious textile experience.

Throughout the fashion for shawls, undecorated twilled weavings of soft blended fibers called "Cashmere" remained popular; sometimes the fabric was natural-colored, sometimes dyed in rich, full color.

Even though Cashmere shawls first appeared in England well before the time of Napoleon, a common misconception persists that they were introduced into Europe by soldiers of Napoleon's campaign in Egypt in 1798–1801. In the heroic Napoleonic paintings of battle action in the Middle East, shawl-like textiles appear as splendid romantic adornment. The uniforms of French officers are bedecked with fluttering sashes and scarfs identifiable as Turkish, Indian, Persian. In numerous portraits of stylish women by Ingres, Gros, and other prominent French painters, Cashmere shawls are depicted with great definition and distinction. The shawls, with their drape and patterns, seem as essential to the expression as do the Oriental carpets in Dutch painting many years earlier. In the portraits, shawls are shown loosely draped, sometimes extending over the furniture as well as the person. They provide a sinuous line moving through the paintings. French fashion drawings of the period illustrate soft cotton dresses complemented by Cashmere shawls that hang loosely around the neck or are caught halfway down the arms, causing the shawl to loop and fall. Or the shawl is slung across one shoulder jauntily or wistfully, or it is held in the hand and allowed to trail along the ground.

The supply of these luxurious shawls could not possibly satisfy the demand. The textiles took very long to weave (a single shawl might take eighteen months); raw materials were scarce. The Indians had not yet learned the methods that later increased and speeded production although changing the shawls. Customers settled on substitutes fabricated to resemble the originals. France was the first to manufacture shawls in imitation of Cashmeres; other countries quickly followed. Domestic copies were often marketed as foreign goods since foreignness was part of the appeal. Even the most conservative and provincial individuals wanted to display touches of the exotic and faraway in the shawls they wore.

(Opposite) Paisley woven shawl, about 1865. The quest is for sinuous curves flowing miraculously from the grid of woven structure. The shawl seems to be a rendered drawing rather than something that evolved from working directly on the loom. It speaks of the compass, ruler and the tools for drafting noncircular curves.
Conspicuously placed within the 4-pointed star of the black center is the white figure imitating the weaver's signature on an Indian shawl. (The Metropolitan Museum of Art, Gift of Mrs. Louis S. Jurist, 1938)

Throughout most of the nineteenth century, these large rectangles of cloth from the looms of Asia and Europe were thrown over whatever sleeves, bodices, crinolines, ruffles and flounces the fashion world favored. Whether the costumes were severe and rigid with bones and wires or natural and sylph-like, the shawls were appropriate—stretched taut around the sculptural figure or draped freely, responsive to movement, providing a sensuous charm. And how convenient shawls were as garments at a time when clothing was not hung in closets but folded on shelves.

Shawls appeared in great variety. Those from faraway places—India, China, Turkey, Persia—were most fashionable. Yet other shawls were also popular. Some were commonplace lengths of woven domestic cloth, coarse homespun devoid of decoration, while others were stripes or plaids. Since these could be woven by any weaver using a simple loom, their production occurred widely, in isolated farm cottages as well as in numerous weaving towns. Fancier shawls were woven in the textile centers; these textiles showed traditional floral patterns closely related to those on European clothing fabrics. Shawls were knitted, embroidered, printed. Cashmeres and Paisleys were part of this fashion impulse.

Paisley is generally thought to have copied its shawls directly from the luxurious Cashmeres. The truth is that imitation Cashmeres had been woven in other places before the town of Paisley started its shawl weaving and that Paisley, entering the field rather late, profited from the experience of other weaving centers and modeled its shawls after those that were successful. The first Paisley shawls, then, were copies of imitations. Later on, the Paisley-type shawls became quite different from the Cashmere shawls that first inspired them as designs conformed to European taste. Since the shawls being woven in India, Persia and Turkey (the whole area was involved in weaving the extremely popular shawls and many were offered as Cashmeres) were changing to meet the requirements of the European market, the Asian and the European shawls kept looking alike. In a remarkable way, the shawls from the two widely different areas kept parallel, although the weaving techniques remained quite different. Sometimes European shawls imitated those being successfully woven in Asia, and sometimes shawls from India, Turkey and Persia imitated those from France and Britain. Great ingenuity and inventiveness were demonstrated by weavers in both areas: the Asians using simple looms and hand processes, the Europeans using ever more complicated monster looms. Because both tried to achieve similar results using radically different tools, the results are of great interest to anyone concerned with the relationship of tool to design.

New York shawl market, 1854. Americans were offered a variety of shawls, from India and China, and from Scotland, England and France. This is "Bulpin's Great Paris Mantilla Emporium and Foreign Shawl Warehouse, New York," as illustrated in United States Magazine of Science, Art, Manufactures, Agriculture, Commerce and Trade, Vol. I, 1854. *(Reproduced from "Fashion, Commerce and Technology in the Nineteenth Century: The Shawl Trade" by Thomas W. Leavitt, in* Textile History, Volume 3)

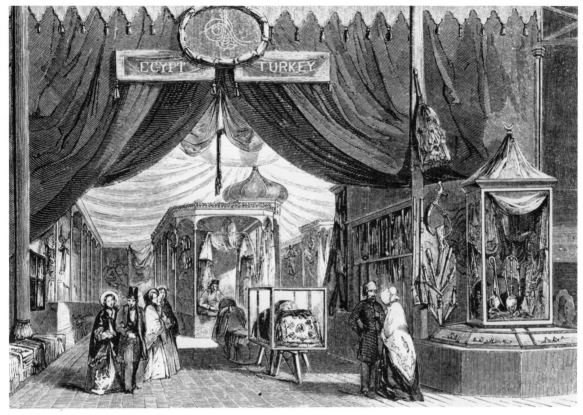

Women wearing patterned shawls at the entrance to the Turkish Department of the great exhibition in London in 1851. (From The Crystal Palace Exhibition, Illustrated Catalogue, *London 1851)*

Embroidered silk crepe shawl, Paisley, about 1830. Shawls from Canton, China, were copied in Paisley. The workmanship of the Scottish embroidery was often comparable to that from China. In some of these shawls, the embroidery was the same color as the background cloth; in others, multi-colors were used for the embellishing. Chinese motives were often injected into woven shawls. (Collection: Paisley Museum and Art Galleries)

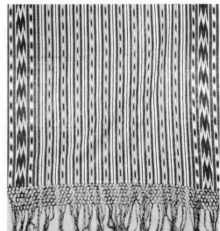

Embroidered Paisley-type shawl, designed to be worn folded to show opposite corners across the wearer's back. The motives from Paisley weavings are clearly stated here, transcribed into embroidered lines, like a drawing, free of the rich color effects that characterized the embroidered Cashmeres and the woven and printed Paisleys. Yet the grey Cashmere fiber on which the embroidery appears has the sensuous touch that so appealed to Europeans when Cashmere shawls first appeared. (Collection: Pat Hickman)

Blue and white cotton scarf imitating a traditional Mexican reboza. Made in Scotland for the Mexican market, mid-nineteenth century. In their zeal to do the world's weaving, the Europeans not only imitated the foreign goods such as Cashmere shawls, which had become fashionable in Europe, they also imitated traditional textiles such as serapes and rebozas to flood the foreign markets. (Crown copyright: Victoria & Albert Museum)

Printed cotton shawl, probably French. This textile, showing the standard distribution of motives, borders, etc., from Cashmere and Paisley-type shawls, was printed with great precision and attention to details. This example was found along with tapa cloths and other native goods in Nive, Savage Islands, Polynesia. At the same time that the famous Paisley shawls were being made, shawls of very different materials, techniques, and patterning were also being manufactured in Paisley and other textile centers, and in towns and villages not remarkable for their textiles. These goods were directed to specific world markets. (Collection: Robert H. Lowie Museum of Anthropology, University of California, Berkeley)

Veil, black hand-run net lace, early nineteenth century American. Pine motives are combined with other motives from Near Eastern textiles. (The Metropolitan Museum of Art, Gift of Mrs. Bonnie W. Leclair, 1925)

22　　　　　　　In Britain, it was the weaving center of Norwich that first imitated Cashmere shawls late in the eighteenth century. The Norwich shawls have a striking clarity of design, which distinguishes them and clearly relates them to the early Cashmeres. Toward the end of the eighteenth century, Norwich was followed by Edinburgh, which produced relatively few shawls; today they are little known (only recently have some authentic Edinburgh shawls appeared). Paisley followed Edinburgh in about 1808. Paisley was already an established weaving center, able to learn from its predecessors in shawl manufacture. Using advanced methods of manufacture and cheap labor, Paisley rapidly seized a large share of the market and drove out competition, until shawls became Paisley's most important industry. Its name was attached to all these shawls wherever woven, so that, today, even Cashmere shawls are often mistakenly referred to as Paisleys.

(Opposite) Jacquard woven shawl, French (?), 1850–60s. Exotic architecture establishes a grid for European vases of full-blown flowers, combined with scenes of pageantry, including a procession of elephants, horses and camels—all suggesting a Hollywood spectacle. In his Handbook of Ornament, *which expresses many of the design preoccupations of Western Europe in the nineteenth century, Franz Sales Meyer recommends, concerning artistic decoration of textile fabrics, "the avoidance of representations of relief, or of perspective views of architecture, which contradict the nature of the flat surface."*

While Cashmere and Paisley-type shawls tend to respect the two-dimensional textile surface, yet three-dimensional effects from various European sources occasionally appear, often amidst the more usual flat shapes. A similar shawl, woven in Paisley about 1840–50, and now in the Paisley Museum, is called "Chinese Fairy-tale Plaid." It includes pagodas, peacocks, human figures, and much exotic vegetation. Such shawls were rare, requiring many fine threads to make possible the weaving of the innumerable details. The Chinese Fairy-tale Plaid is said to have required 150,000 shots of weft, and 180 warps per inch. (Crown copyright: Victoria & Albert Museum)

Corner of a woven silk shawl, Britain 1810–20. The tip of the cone is a large flower, while the cone itself is a formal flower and leaves surrounded by a trailing floral arrangement defining the cone. The borders are bold, flowing flower forms. Everything is without the delicate detail that characterized later shawls. The scale of the pattern suggests drawloom weaving quite unlike the Jacquard weaving that was done later. (Crown copyright: Victoria & Albert Museum)

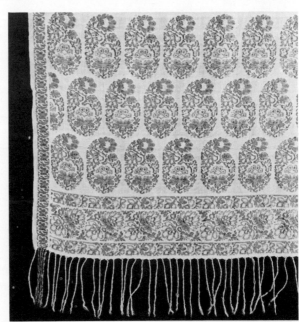

Since shawls from Paisley cannot be distinguished with certainty from those woven in other European centers (although they can be distinguished from most of the Asian ones because of the differences in weaving techniques), all the European shawls are referred to here as "Paisley-type," unless a specific derivation is known. Only shawls known to be from the town of Paisley are called Paisleys. Consistency would require that the Cashmere shawls be referred to as Cashmere-type, since many of them were woven in places far from Kashmir; yet, for the sake of convenience, all are here referred to as Cashmeres. (In accordance with current practice, the area of India where the Cashmere shawls were woven is spelled "Kashmir" while the textiles are spelled "Cashmeres" and the fiber is "Cashmere.")

Shawls kept changing to conform to rapidly changing fashions. By the middle of the nineteenth century, crinolines had become so enlarged that two women, each wearing one, could not comfortably move in a small drawing room at the same time, while a man was obliged to exercise the greatest skill and agility, and "go through almost acrobatic contortions,"[4] to walk arm in arm with a lady, ever fearful of treading on her crinoline. This extravagant display of textiles was reflected in the shawls themselves and not only in their size. Long rectangular shawls rather than squares became popular, while textures became increasingly heavy, dense and substantial rather than lightweight and diaphanous, as earlier shawls had been. The new generous proportions encouraged skilled designers to indulge in ever more intricate and involved patterns that were quite unprecedented in world textiles and certainly far different from the rather austere Cashmere shawls that originally inspired the fashion. Paisley-type designs became a unique textile expression.

Early Paisley shawls showed simple isolated motives surrounded by open areas and small patterned borders. Because looms at that time were unable to weave the large patterned textiles in one piece, components were woven separately and later sewed together by women in the Paisley area. Gradually, when improvements in the loom permitted larger weavings, shawls were woven in one piece, isolated motives expanded and became enmeshed, and borders reached out, crowding the edges and moving inward toward the center. With the new Jacquard mechanism, an invention in 1805 that allowed warp threads to be raised by the operation of punched cards, the patterning increased even further in the European shawls. The Cashmeres kept pace through combinations of weaving and embroidering. In many cases the shawls—both the Paisley-type and the Cashmeres—ended up as an indulgence in complex pattern and technical ingenuity. They became exhibitionistic in their complications. If the European looms could be made to perform wonders, those wonders were offered to a delighted public. The weavers of Kashmir were obliged to keep pace.

Eighteenth century cape, made up in Europe from cloth painted in India. When such patterned cotton became fashionable, imitations were made in Europe using blockprints to speed the process. Quite unlike the shawls, which retained the rectangle of loom weaving, this garment is assembled from various strips to form a large oval. Patterns are not matched but appear in chance juxtapositions that do not respect the intentions of those who painted the cloth. The shawls that replaced such outer garments were uncut rectangles that, when they hung in folds, created constantly changing patterns. (Crown copyright: Victoria & Albert Museum)

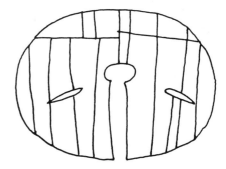

26

Jacquard Paisley-type shawl. Seen from the back, a woman appeared encased in a textile reaching from her neck to her ankles. Textile compositions of elaborate, unrepeated motives were displayed like heraldic symbols or emblems. The costumes were not too unlike the ''moving paintings'' of Japanese kimonos or Chinese dragon robes or religious vestments. Paisleys enclosed the woman in borders surrounding patterns elaborating an axis like the human spine. To display the wondrous textile patterns never seen before, ''plaids'' were folded across the center, while ''squares'' were folded diagonally. (Collection: Pat Hickman)

Although the later shawls showed patterns to satisfy European taste, they were, nevertheless, quite unlike the clothing fabrics that had been fashionable in Europe for cutting and reassembling by seamstresses and tailors. Patterns on dress fabrics implied endless movement in all directions, with motives repeated regularly down the length of the cloth. These patterns were then subject to the juxtapositions that occurred through cutting and reassembling; the patterns were transformed according to how they were put together into garments. They never appeared exactly as they did on the loom. By contrast, the shawls were more like rugs, bedspreads and tablecloths, and like the saris, sarongs, etc., of other cultures. Each shawl was a complete unit, a composition of motives enclosed by borders. Through all their mutations over the years, the shawls seldom lost their clear identification with textiles from non-European countries, where textiles were used as they came from the loom rather than as shaped pieces that were cut and reassembled.

The non-European identification of Paisley-type shawls derived, too, from the design motive that originally had been copied from the Cashmere shawls and that persisted prominently. It is often referred to as the pine or cone, and known in India as *Buta*, meaning flower. This became the Paisley motive, the "Paisley." Throughout all the years of the shawl's popularity, this motive appeared extended, compressed, superimposed, intertwined, elaborated in every conceivable way while remaining recognizable. For a short while, an attempt was made to replace this motive with decorative foliage, but the effort failed and the familiar Paisley reasserted itself. Paisley designs remained when the shawls disappeared.

The Paisley motive or pine motive. Here it is elongated, superimposed, and embellished with floral extensions. The design is rendered on squared paper with notations for enlarging. (Collection: Paisley Museum and Art Galleries)

While shawl patterns resembled rugs and bedspreads, shawls were always perceived by their designers in relation to the human figure and perceived also as something not flat but three-dimensional and moving in space. The patterns, which sometimes appear rather mechanical and static and overly composed when laid out flat, changed and attained their dynamism through draping.

The number of different shawl patterns is astonishing. Among the shawls that have been preserved by chance, two are seldom alike. (Who could have predicted which shawls would remain 100 years after they were made? Those fabricated with such fanfare for Queen Victoria can not be traced today, while many that were carried across hostile lands and seas have found a safe haven in museums.) To the women who wore the shawls, the differences were obvious and of paramount importance. Over the years, there were white-centered plaids, black-centered plaids, long red shawls, black border shawls, Thibet shawls, green-centered shawls, zebra plaids, reversible shawls, compartment plaids, Canton crepes, chenille, Angola and many others. The Angola, an imitation Cashmere made of Angora, tended to shed its fibers and consequently was unpopular with gentlemen escorts. If a woman could afford more than one shawl, she had a heavy plaid for cold weather and a white- or scarlet-centered shawl for summer. Because Queen Victoria preferred the plaid—the long rectangle—few fashionable women chose the square.

A publication of the time declared, "We scarcely know a truer test of a gentlewoman's taste in dress than her selection of a Shawl and her manner of wearing it."[5] Customers could even choose separate components—centers, borders and fringes—that would be made up into a "dressmaker's shawl." Borders woven in France might be combined with centers woven in Britain.

Paisley shawls were usually woven from wool and silk, although some were all silk. After 1840, some were all wool, some were cotton. They were not the flowing textiles of the early Cashmeres. After all, the Cashmere fiber was not available in any quantity and could not be duplicated. Only a few special shawls were woven in Paisley from imported Cashmere wool. Fashion requirements had changed since early in the nineteenth century when the diaphanous was so engaging. Because they were expected to be warm, protective, and durable, Paisley-type shawls could be relatively thick. The wool and silk, and the thickness, were of utmost significance in the creation of the complex color effects and intricate patterns that characterize these textiles. The wool and silk fibers gave designers the full, rich colors unknown to other dyed fibers such as cotton and linen , while the thickness permitted the inclusion and manipulation of multitudes of fine threads required by intricate woven patterns. The many fine threads stimulated the diversity of designs.

The diversity of Paisley designs was also encouraged by the methods of weaving the shawls. A loom was threaded or programmed for a specific design. The loom could then weave only that pattern, until a new pattern was threaded in—a laborious and extremely time-consuming process. Modifications in color were, of course, possible without changing the threading. Since the weaving was a slow process, especially early in the industry, a single loom could produce relatively few shawls in a year, perhaps only three or four. A shawl might take six months to weave, four of the months being spent in enlarging the design and programming the loom. Consequently, very many looms were required, each weaving a small quota of shawls. Theoretically, each of these many looms could have been programmed for a different design. Sometimes, when a shawl was commissioned by members of the royal family, no more than a single shawl was woven from a design.

With many looms weaving many different patterns, a multitude of tastes could be satisfied. Old established patterns were woven year after year to satisfy a conservative demand at the same time that other looms were weaving the latest designs, fabricating them quickly as possible to please the adventurous.

The nineteenth century was a critical and confusing time in the history of costume and fashion. While some critics interpret it as a time emphasizing the different grades of the social hierarchy by clearly defined differences of dress, others describe it as the democratization of costume, especially in Britain. Although women of wealth and position devoted their lives to distinctions in dress, democratic ideals aimed at minimizing differences in social standing and wealth rather than accentuating them. What is certain is that women of even moderate means were seeing the possibilities of wearing fashionable dress and reflecting fashion changes in what they wore.

Fancy shawls offered such a range of quality and prices that rich and poor could buy them. Shawls with full colors and patterns varied from the luxurious and expensive Cashmeres of India to the printed and cheap cotton imitations. In between were the woven shawls of Paisley, Norwich, Edinburgh and numerous other places. Early in the industry, Paisley shawls especially were in the luxury class of dress. Differences between the expensive and the cheap shawls allowed the upper classes to be secure in the knowledge that their shawls were superior by merely touching them. At the same time, the similarities in appearance allowed everyone to feel part of the same fashion impulse. Since the shawls were rectangular pieces of cloth, unfitted and uncontoured, they were in fact ready-made, ready-to-wear clothing, perfect for the new surge toward mass production. To a great extent, one size fitted all.

30

Paisley woodcut for printing shawls by hand. Patterns with fine details requiring block surfaces with metal insets. Blocks varied in size from border blocks only three or four inches long to blocks twelve-inches square. Large blocks were very heavy, extremely difficult to manipulate with precision in registering, or positioning, the blocks. (Collection: Paisley Museum and Art Galleries)

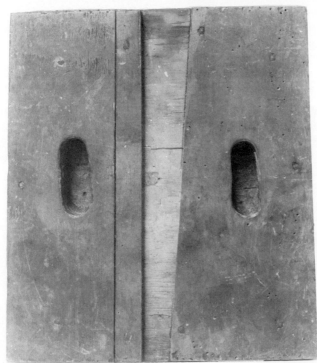

Back of a wooden printing block used in Paisley. The holes are for holding the block, allowing it to be easily held in various positions. (Collection: Paisley Museum and Art Galleries)

About 1870 the shawls became outmoded; they became victims of the democratization they represented. They were thought of as clothing for the working classes. In many instances, the woven shawls had been driven out or replaced by cheap printed imitations. Before this time, when printed textiles imitated scarce or expensive weavings, the woven variety continued to be regarded as superior and more desirable. With Paisleys, the circumstances were different. As the shawls grew more and more monumental in their dimensions to match the proportions of the costumes, the weight kept increasing, growing burdensome. The woven shawls could not be lightened without discarding the distinctive patterning—a problem that for years had concerned the Paisley weavers.

Printed shawls of lightweight and even sheer materials could show the traditional colors and patterns while possessing the added advantages of being cheap and fast to produce. Shawls printed on light cotton and silk were ideal for summer, much cooler than the heavy woolen shawls. A woman could afford several printed shawls and experience variety in her dress. The lightness and cheapness were in tune with the new times. More than that, the printed shawls had an undeniable charm, a wonder of their own. Special sheer fabrics were woven as backgrounds for the printed patterns. The final results were often remarkable for the subtle relationship of weaving and printing, for a sensation of color and texture overlaid with patterns. Design motives that had for a long time been familiar as substantial wool constructions of astonishing complexity appeared in a different guise of floating transparency, so familiar and yet so unfamiliar, so like, and yet so unlike the woven designs that had begun to seem heavy, ponderous and eternal.

Printed Paisley silk shawl. This blockprinted shawl is without the refinement that is often associated with silk patterns. It seems surprisingly offhand, almost a parody of the woven designs that inspired it. Printed Paisley shawls can be divided into two kinds: those that imitate woven shawls and those that use shawl motives for independent expressions. From a distance, and from a photograph, many of the imitations cannot be distinguished from the woven models. Weavers are reported to have suffered a serious blow in 1850 when printed shawls appeared as competition. Until then, printed shawls were luxury items, expensive goods of silk and wool. After that, they were often cheap cotton. When cheap printed shawls became popular with the ''mill girls,'' the sales of all shawls were affected. Shawls could no longer be high fashion, a status symbol among the wealthy. (Collection: Paisley Museum and Art Galleries)

(Above) Printed Paisley shawl. Some printed shawls show enormous care in positioning numerous blocks for splendid color effects, while others display prints careless in their dyeing and slipshod in their placement, quite unrelated to the cloth on which they appear. Sometimes the poor printed shawls and the cheap woven ones have remarkable vitality, while refined shawls are often static and lifeless. A detail of considerable interest in printed shawls is the fitting together of the blocks at the corners. Even when shawls imitated woven models, improvisations were necessary at the corners. The care devoted to changing directions and making motives fit together persuasively indicates the concern with producing quality textiles. Here, the large outer borders butt together without any contrivance, while the small inner border is beveled. Printed diagonal lines recall the twill of woven shawls, while short verticals edging the narrow borders suggest the patching of Cashmere shawls. (Collection: Paisley Museum and Art Galleries)

Printed shawls were made in Paisley along with the woven variety. Paisley was not only a weaving center, it was a *textile* center known for its printing, dyeing, embroidering, fringing, bleaching, etc., as well as for its weaving. Whatever was required for producing textiles was available in Paisley. To this one community were attracted all the textile skills, and also the commercial resources for financing, distributing, and merchandising. Just as Paisley entered the weaving of shawls late, it began printing shawls after printing had been done elsewhere; and then Paisley profited by others' experience and made improvements in what had already been done. Today little attention is paid to the printed shawls and their relationship to the well-known woven variety. While many of the late printed shawls remain, few of the early ones were preserved. Those on silk gauze became brittle and they were discarded. Yet the printed shawls are known to have developed and changed along with the woven shawls and to have exerted a profound and continuing influence on printed textile design worldwide.

Both the printed and woven Paisley-type shawls are transitional works: between hand and machine processes of production. Both reflect the economic and social changes that stirred the nineteenth century. Both express the same will to experiment in order to achieve abundant production of beautiful textiles, to satisfy the demands of a rapidly changing society.

When hard times finally struck toward the end of the century, the Paisley workers tried desperately to survive. They continued to change their designs and to improve their equipment. The kinds of changes that had characterized the industry from its beginning and had kept the shawls fashionably different for so many years continued to be made even after no hope remained for the industry. The collapse of the shawl industry is blamed on the Franco-Prussian war; the bustle; the cheap woven and printed varieties made for the working classes. Finally, shawls became something only for old ladies and the poor. Even in remote country villages, the shawls were considered old-fashioned. When the industry collapsed altogether, methods and skills were quickly forgotten. The weavers were dispersed and the looms were destroyed.

(Opposite) Printed Paisley shawl. Although the pattern does not meet precisely along the diagonal joining of the blocks, the irregularities are lost in the dense patterning. (Collection: Paisley Museum and Art Galleries)

2. The Town

How the shawls happened to be woven there

The Scotland of several centuries ago seems too contradictory for an outsider to comprehend. At the same time that it appears strife-torn, hostile, isolated, and thoroughly undeveloped (Samuel Johnson's descriptions of his travels through Scotland in 1773 create a most disturbing image of desperate people emigrating—shiploads escaping hopeless conditions), Scotland displays truly startling qualities—cultural attainments and refinements, and a lively intellectual exchange with England and the Continent. When Scotland became a modern industrial society, the transformation was rapid, forced. Dislocations were extreme, with all the evidence left standing. The shawl industry is part of that puzzling Scottish scene.

The two largest cities in Scotland are in the south. Edinburgh is on the East Coast looking toward the North Sea and the ports of the Continent. Glasgow is twenty-five miles inland from the West Coast, facing the Irish Sea and the "New World." On a map, both cities appear to be located toward the center of the island. Now that they are well connected by highway and railroad, the distance between them seems negligible. I recently heard of a high spot in Glasgow with a view of Edinburgh. I can not confirm its existence, yet the sense of this possibility suggests the nearness. Because they seem so close together and yet are clearly related to opposite coasts, the awareness of Britain as a small island is very affecting.

The two cities were formerly not so close. At the time when the shawls were first woven in Paisley, the trip of forty-six miles from Glasgow to Edinburgh took four and a half hours. This was a remarkable improvement over the situation only fifty years earlier, when the journey took twelve hours by stagecoach or two days by cart. The roads were in a desperate condition although they were improved over what they had been shortly before, when they were too primitive for wheeled vehicles and the common way to carry goods was on horseback. Scotland lingered far longer than England in woeful conditions of travel. Vast areas were without the contacts, influences and stimulation that accompany decent means of communication.

Detail, American coverlet, nineteenth century. Many Scottish weavers, disillusioned by poverty and hard times, became immigrants to the United States and Canada. Often they no longer wove. But some continued using their skills to produce patterned textiles. This formal arrangement of motives includes Paisleys set together with thistle-like flowers, surrounded by branches moving into the open field, exactly as they did in the shawl designs. The weaving technique is not like the Paisley shawl technique. (Collection: Program in Visual Design, University of California, Berkeley)

As long as the commercial contacts were with England and the Continent, Edinburgh was dominant. Influences filtered to Glasgow via the capital, which was Scotland's center of learning and the leader of its industrial advances. When commercial orientation developed toward the American colonies, and following Scotland's union with England, Glasgow was in a geographical position to become the new great center of commerce.

Glasgow dominates a Lowland area known as the West of Scotland. It is not the flat area that "Lowland" suggests, but is an uneven landscape of valleys, streams and woods. Only fifty years before the start of the shawl industry, the West of Scotland was an agricultural countryside with half the population living in tiny hamlets. Flax was grown, spun, woven and bleached as part of a domestic industry—Scotland's chief industry.

Paisley is close to Glasgow, in a valley with the River Cart running through. Today, the river seems an almost incidental feature in a congested urban area of over 100,000. From very early times, Paisley differed from the surrounding towns and hamlets. While it began as an agricultural settlement like many others, it changed with the founding of a monastery there in the twelfth century. In 1219, the monastery became Paisley Abbey. Craftsmen settled near the Abbey to satisfy its needs; visitors made pilgrimages there. Other visitors were attracted to Paisley because the town was on a main line of communication between Glasgow and Ayrshire, where pilgrims went to visit the very important Shrine and Abbey of Whithorn. Gradually, during the period of the Middle Ages, Paisley became a center of fine craftsmen working for the monastery, a market, and a halting place on a much traveled route.

As the town prospered, weavers from the area were attracted there: from Ayrshire and the nearby counties, even from Edinburgh. Because the town seemed prosperous, Highlanders moved down, while the Irish chose Paisley as a place to emigrate and take up plain weaving while their children were apprenticed to fancy weavers. An influx of workers occurred early in the eighteenth century, when Glasgow's trade with the New World grew. Yet Paisley, until the mid 1700's, was a small weaving settlement; the dramatic change took place after 1750.

Scotland had become known for coarse woven linens that were cheap and often inferior. Apparently, the cheapness and coarseness accounted for the early success of the Scottish linen industry, for the goods could find a market in the English plantations. Scotland desperately needed goods to export since it required so many imported goods. Because the woven linens were such important items in the Scottish economy, the government tried to increase and improve production and to enforce standards of quality. A Board of Manufacture was appointed in 1727 to encourage industry in Scotland, especially the linen industry.

Textile methods on the Continent were studied and reported on. Grants were given to encourage the growing of flax and the laying out of bleachfields. Dutch and Irish bleachers, and skilled Irish weavers, were attracted to Scotland. French cambric weavers came to set up a school in Edinburgh. Housewives were offered prizes for the best woven cloth. When foreign weavers came to teach their skills, the men taught weaving while the wives demonstrated the ways of spinning fine yarn. Spinning schools were established. Methods of making linen thread were introduced from Holland. (The making of thread was ultimately to become the town's principal industry; Paisley became the thread capitol of the world.)

While Glasgow was becoming Britain's leading linen town, Paisley was earning a growing reputation for fine linen—lawns, cambrics, and damasks, some with extremely complex patterning. This reputation undoubtedly led to an event of great consequence for Paisley's future as a manufacturer of shawls: a silk industry was established there. With the introduction of silk, Paisley emerged as a textile center of international importance.

A silk industry had grown up during the second half of the seventeenth century in the district of London called Spitalfields. This place attracted master weavers from France at a time when they were escaping religious persecution. Spitalfields profited from the know-how of these and other craftsmen and was soon famous for patterned silks: brocaded taffetas, satins, and damasks similar to those woven in Lyon, the great center of the French silk industry. When these heavy silks with their large patterns went out of fashion, Spitalfields turned to patterned silk shawls.

In 1759 a branch of this silk trade from Spitalfields was established at Paisley, where silk weaving "was brought to such perfection especially in the light and more fanciful kinds, that in a short time Paisley silks almost rivaled those of France."[6] Paisley silks were said to be prized over those of Spitalfields; they were fashionable throughout Europe. Paisley became known especially for silk gauze—a sheer silk in a crossed warp technique—and this provided employment for thousands of workers in and around the town. When the trade in silk gauze declined, shawl manufacture was undertaken, following the lead of Spitalfields and other weaving centers. As they had done before, Paisley weavers turned their skills from one product to another. The silk gauzes were to reappear as cloth for printing Paisley shawls when lightweight printed shawls became fashionable.

Wherever silk was introduced—in China, Persia, India, Italy, France—remarkable energy and inventiveness went into exploring the potentials of the loom. The looms, which Italy inherited from the East and which wove the splendid silks of Venice, Lucca, and Pisa, made their way to Lyon, then to London and Canterbury, and finally to Paisley. Along with the looms went traditions of craftsmanship, standards of textile quality, and a spirit of exploration and change. Ways of textile production came to Paisley ready-made, having been developed and perfected over many years in other places. Fabrics woven elsewhere provided models for the Paisley weavers, who were willing, boldly and often ruthlessly, to take the next step. It is possible to interpret Paisley shawls as traditional European silks rendered in wool—as the product of the centuries of investigations and experiments that followed the introduction of silk. The silk industry laid the foundation for the shawl trade.

Samples from a Muslin and Gauze Pattern Book, *from the firm of Brown and Sharp. These textiles were being woven in Paisley at about the time the shawl industry started. The book is dated 1770, but some samples are as late as 1816. The cloth was for silk handkerchiefs and cotton gauze robes. Samples in the book are described as sprigged silk gauze, striped silk gauze, gossamer gauze, pearl spider soft silk net, silk gauze lappet, harness gauze. Lappet and harness describe special looms used for mechanical patterns. The well-known shawls were woven on harness looms. For a while, some shawls were woven on lappet looms; they are mentioned from 1818 to 1819. The sample in the lower right corner shows special dyeing of some of the yarns; this technique relates to the special dyeing of warps for the shawls. (Collection: Paisley Museum and Art Galleries)*

(Right) Afternoon dress, 1825–30. The model wears a silk gauze shawl and carries an embroidered handkerchief. Both articles could have been made in Paisley. Its silk gauzes were fashionable throughout Britain and the Continent for shoulder scarfs and handkerchiefs. Its fine cotton muslin, flowered by women in the area, were fashionable for handkerchiefs, aprons, collars, scarfs, etc. In weaving these fancy textiles, Paisley weavers addressed technical problems that were encountered later in the famous shawls: heavy decorative borders enclosing plain fields; transitional motives relating borders to fields, etc. Some sheer cloth woven in Paisley showed patterns with the floats clipped on the back to keep the floats from showing through. The weavers were later to use this shearing technique for shawls to get rid of excess yarns. (Crown copyright: Victoria & Albert Museum)

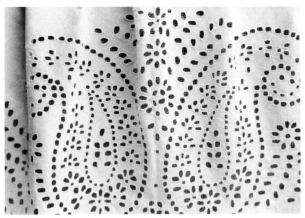

(Above) Ayrshire embroidery, also called Ayrshire needlework, about 1840. Paisley motives are embroidered in eyelets. Fine cotton muslin was woven and stamped in Paisley to be embroidered by women in Ayrshire and Northern Ireland. The workers who "figured" muslin were called "tambourers" or "tambouring girls" because they held their work in tambours or frames. These women were also called "flowerers" because the common motives that they added to the muslin were sprigs of flowers. Some of the finest examples of white work were baptismal garments. Many were cherished as family treasures and have been preserved. (Collection: Paisley Museum and Art Galleries)

When commerce with the New World brought cotton as a raw fiber for the Scottish textile industry, Glasgow and the surrounding area—so favorably situated for trade with the United States—became the center of cotton manufacture in Scotland. Linen manufacture moved elsewhere. Along with specialization in fine cotton yarn and fine cloth for export came calico printing and embroidering. Paisley identified itself with refined needlework. Flemish immigrants brought the technique of "tambouring," which became a domestic employment for women in the area. A length of cloth was stretched on a large rectangular frame with rollers on each end. The embroiderers worked from both sides of the frame. In the 1850's, at the height of the industry, 5000 women in Paisley were employed in the work (often done as piece work) in the home—dotting and flowering muslin.

Paisley's reputation and its prosperity encouraged a flow of un-skilled immigrants—cheap labor. People in such desperate straits could be exploited to turn out products competitive in the world's markets. Merchants parcelled out work to weavers in a wide area, using Paisley as headquarters. Work was also put out to those able to spin, fringe, sew, embroider. Warehouses, credit facilities, merchants and capital were at hand for such commercial enterprises. Being so favorably situated near the West Coast, the town could bring raw materials from great distances to convert into textiles for export; the variety of materials—linen, wool, cotton, silk—gave Paisley many options in what it could produce and also options for change. The landscape allowed bleachfields to be established in the flat river lands and dye works and print fields to be set up along the banks of the waterways. Open spaces were convenient for the expansion of houses, factories and mills. And all the while, Paisley enjoyed close connections with the new industrial center of Glasgow, which was expanding at such an amazing rate to become Scotland's greatest commercial center and the Second City of the Empire.

With its international connections, Paisley could respond to the rapid changes in fashion and taste that characterized the eighteenth and nineteenth centuries. When shawls became the rage, Paisley was ready, in fact eager, since its silk gauze trade was declining. Paisley could profit from the shawl-making experience of Norwich, Edinburgh, London and the various weaving centers of France, learning from their ways and copying their models, then initiating its own improvements and methods, until the name of Paisley became synonymous with similar shawls wherever produced.

I studied with much interest the photographs of nineteenth century Paisley and also the very moving photographs of street scenes of Glasgow from the same period. Paisley of the photographs does not fit the town I once envisaged; it seems closer to Glasgow as I first saw it (and reminiscent of

Chicago as I remember it from rather early in this century) with its undeniable feel of an industrial city, the landscape transformed by industry, the river running heavily between industrial buildings.

The engravings of Paisley made in the eighteenth century are something else. They show a pleasant town set in hills and trees. The rooftops appear out of the dense foliage. There is a feeling of sky. A row of thatched cottages where the artisans lived moves through the vegetation. It is all like a romantic painting by John Constable—the sense of intimacy with nature, the habitations pleasantly complementing nature. In an aquatint showing the town in 1825, when the shawl industry was in full swing, the artist I. Clark chose to draw a panorama with the town spread out at some distance, quite similar to the earlier engravings with hills and foliage in the foreground. But now the town itself, while it still had its spires and pointed rooftops, was enclosed with mills and warehouses and industrial chimneys. In the foreground were apparent developers and planners surveying the remaining empty spaces for expansion of the town.

Paisley in 1767. Although the town was already a lively textile center, the scene is pleasantly bucolic, truly idyllic. Rows of cottages are set amidst foliage. (Engraved by R. Paul. Courtesy: Paisley Museum and Art Galleries)

Paisley in 1825 shows the new expansion, the congestion, and the developers planning more. They seem to be confidently charting a brave new world. (Drawn by I. Clark. Courtesy: Paisley Museum and Art Galleries)

In all the photographs of Victorian Paisley, nature has vanished— no trees, no foliage. It is as though the surrounding hills have been leveled, so absent are they from the photographers' compositions. About everything is a greyness, a black sootiness. The inclemencies of the weather seem no longer to produce the lush greenery, but merely heavy, sunless air. The people on the streets express an enormous sense of isolation; they seem quite separate from their surroundings.

From looking at the Victorian photographs, it is not hard to believe that at the height of its industrial growth—including the years of the shawl manufacture—the streets of Paisley were dumping grounds for all manner of filth and ill-smelling refuse. Hens, ducks, geese and pigs fed in the garbage. Streets, reputedly the narrowest in the country, had open drains. Rivers as well were unclean. Use of the waterways for dyeing and bleaching, and for manufacturing, polluted and diminished the town's supplies. These conditions, combined with the overcrowding and the miserable living conditions for the poor, encouraged diseases of all types. Epidemics of cholera occurred, and serious outbreaks of typhus, smallpox, and enteric fever. Paisley was known as the dirtiest town in Scotland, the most unhealthy town in Scotland.

Contradictory images emerge: a dreary corrupted environment of filth and disease; extreme poverty and overcrowding; exploited workers desperately surviving; a lovely landscape; a town preoccupied with textiles; men, women and children involved with fiber in all its aspects; weavers writing poetry, engaging in political arguments, enjoying their gardens and pets. The two images refuse to coalesce into a single image; they exist simultaneously, neither quite persuasive.

I wanted the shawls to be products of the thatched cottages set in the splendid landscapes of the eighteenth century engravings rather than the dreary factory town of the nineteenth century photographs. I keep insisting to myself that, although the shawls were woven in the nineteenth century, they were truly a product of the preceding centuries. I take comfort in this thought, although I do not quite convince myself. The desperate life of the weavers in the latter part of the nineteenth century contrasted with the life of relative affluence in the earlier century, which encouraged a confidence, a time for discussion, for reading, for enjoyment of life. The weavers of the late nineteenth century were ground down to a desperate subsistence, crushed by a series of desperate economic crises involving power looms and surplus of labor and a product no longer in demand.

I once saw a small book showing a map of Paisley delicately sketched. The names of Gauze Street, Cotton Street, Shuttle Street, Thread Street, and others, were delightful, especially as inscribed on the map—hesitantly, tremblingly. Seen on the signs in a modern town, a single name seemed unexceptional. In isolation, the words Thread and Shuttle and Cotton became only convenient references to modern streets. They seemed unable to even recall that this had been a great textile center, that a great textile flowering had occurred there such a short time ago. But the succession of names, one

When the small market town became a great textile center—the third town in Scotland—the lovely River Cart and the surrounding landscape were transformed. This photograph taken in 1858 at Lonend, Paisley, shows the town's old towers and spires in the distance. (Photograph: Rob Russell. Courtesy: Paisley Museum and Art Galleries)

Paisley in 1977 showing Silk Street, the name left over from the town's years as a great textile center.

after another, in such proximity, began to define and perpetuate the weaving section of Paisley, although the buildings and the weavers were gone. I experienced a sense of place. I could easily have spent time with the old maps, studying the town of the eighteenth and nineteenth centuries, locating the old bleaching fields, the cottage rows, the dyeing areas, the canal and coach routes.

Instead I experienced the modern town on a Saturday morning. When I first saw it, the streets seemed infused with a special energy. The thing to do on Saturday morning was to shop, to move on the streets, as a family occupation. Probably this had been the pattern for decades. Suddenly I realized that reading about the West of Scotland was altogether different from being there. The vitality of the place, even at the height of the shawl production, was never communicated to me in the writings. The shawl industry could be understood only by experiencing the vitality of the modern town alongside, intermeshed with, modern Glasgow. For the remarkable energy that extended along the bus route from Glasgow to Paisley on a Saturday morning seemed to extend also from one century to the next, despite the long hardships that followed the high development of the industrial revolution. The whole area lost its economic momentum but somehow energy remained: like the massive sooty Victorian buildings in Glasgow and the street names in Paisley, like the energy that is said to linger perceptibly around the ancient megaliths.

Being familiar with the sprawl of American cities and the desecrations of the landscape surrounding urban centers, I was struck by the abruptness with which the city became unspoiled countryside—Lowlands became Highlands, with all that the words have come to mean.

The contrast between Glasgow's urban area known as Central Clydeside, with its lively industry and commerce, and the natural beauties so close at hand recalled Sir Walter Scott's novel, *Rob Roy*, in which he shifts rapidly from urban life in Glasgow to the rough life in the surrounding landscape. He wrote the novel in 1817, at the time the shawl production was getting underway in Paisley. Although he set the action 100 years earlier, he expressed the concerns of his own century. At the time he was writing, Glasgow was experiencing the new industrialization, while the Highlands remained as they remain today to a remarkable degree—natural and unspoiled. In the novel, city existence—the machine and the machine-like—contrast with the romantic life in the wild countryside that Scott loved. The loom represents the machine; the industrial life that it fostered is the machine-like. The Highlander reviles the city man as someone "wi' accounts, and yarn winnules, and looms, and shuttles, like a mere mechanical person." He is contemptuous of "weavers and spinners and sic-like mechanical persons and their pursuits."[7]

By experiencing the proximity of Paisley to Glasgow I sensed what I should have known: that the same powerful forces of change—of commerce and industry—that had transformed Glasgow also stirred Paisley. And that the lovely shawls woven by hand in Paisley cottages were understandable only in the context of the ferment known as the industrial revolution. For the first time, I could almost believe that a Scottish town produced the textiles that took its name.

Only twenty-five years after the last Paisley shawl was woven, Matthew Blair, a Paisley native who was brought up in the shawl trade, could write that the very memory of the industry was well-nigh lost. When he wrote about the grand old Paisley weavers who were friends and instructors of his youth, he said that the weavers were almost extinct and that the present generation in Paisley was engaged in other and more varied occupations, which perhaps accounted for the town's being one of the most prosperous in the kingdom. Blair became acquainted with the shawl trade when it was on the decline; he witnessed its decay and extinction, with the consequent distress and unemployment. The best years for weavers in Paisley were the years of weaving silks and fancy cottons, and the early years of the shawl trade. In those times, Blair says, weavers were to some degree their own designers—they worked out their ideas on their looms. They worked out ways to adapt their looms to accomplish new fabrics. Vast mechanical skill was exercised by these weavers in a series of inventions now forgotten. The year 1820, according to Blair's reckoning, was the culminating point of the ingenuity and skill of the handweavers. They were workmen who, he says, for general intelligence have no counterpart today. Many were said to have had libraries equal to those of ministers and professional men. The occupation of weaving was favorable to intellectual development. Later a division of labor and the use of mechanical appliances kept the weavers from exercising these abilities. With the Jacquard attachment, a new type of workman appeared; the old cultured and ingenious weaver gradually disappeared.

As long as the shawls were woven, from about 1800 to 1878, the designs changed, the methods of manufacture changed and the conditions in the town of Paisley changed. A statement made regarding Paisley in the early years might not be at all true later on. Yet, throughout the years, the shawls seem to form a coherent body as a single textile expression. This fact has probably encouraged generalizations and simplifications about aspects that are neither general nor simple.

3. The Weavers

And the cottages where they wove

In 1964 I visited the town of Paisley to see the museum that was listed as having an exhibition of shawls, working drawings, and a loom. I wanted to see the place where the shawls were woven, even though I knew that their manufacture had ceased long ago. I could never quite believe that Paisley shawls were woven in a town in Scotland.

A special quality of a handwoven textile such as a Paisley shawl is its ability to evoke an awareness that someone, someplace, wove it. When a handwoven textile is known to have been made decades or centuries ago, and

46

(Opposite) Two weavers standing beside a dismantled loom. Some of the old looms were converted to Jacquards, while others were destroyed. The weavers wear scarves against the cold, and aprons to protect the weaving. (Messrs. Ritchie and Cornell in 1883. Courtesy: Paisley Museum and Art Galleries)

when it is held in the hand and not merely seen, time becomes like the space looked across when viewing a panorama. Curiously, the intervening time, like the intervening space in a panorama, clarifies. The years provide a focus; they are a telescope for comprehending a distant object. Awareness is sharpened and a sense of wholeness of the textile in relation to a life, a society, is instilled. Then the enjoyment of a historical textile becomes more than an analysis of the structure. It becomes more, too, than an aesthetic response to colors and patterns skillfully contrived. Once the someone-ness of a textile is sensed, even though the individual creator must forever be anonymous—and perhaps partly because of that circumstance—everything surrounding the creation of the textile becomes animated. The textile speaks not of a life, but of life.

When Samuel Johnson made his famous journey through Scotland with James Boswell only a few years before the start of the shawl industry, he described the landscape, resources, population, transportation, commercial enterprise. Nothing corresponded with what seemed essential to a place about to become known for a product often identified with the new machine society. Sir Walter Scott's romantic novels made the shawl production in Scotland quite as unlikely as did Johnson's travelogue.

Knowing Scotland's textiles only as tartans and well-publicized tweeds from remote islands, I was compelled, in order to account for the

shawls, to reconcile a rural image with a thoroughly sophisticated urban product. I fancied modern Paisley to be isolated, like a mining town of the American West that had enjoyed a brief but brilliant heyday and then had lingered on into another century as a dusty tourist trap.

The plane from the United States dropped me in Glasgow on its way to Copenhagen. Approached in this way, Glasgow seemed as remote as Greenland and Iceland, which I had seen from the plane only a few minutes before. The landscape from the airport was overwhelmingly green; apparently the juicy luxuriance had more to do with the abundance of rainfall than with unusual fertility of the soil. Set in this fresh, lovely garden was Glasgow—alas, a bleak industrial city left over from another century. Despite the copious evidence in the soot, I could not believe that Glasgow had recently been of major consequence in the development of the modern world. How could the ingenuity and inventiveness, the thought and creative enterprise that characterized the Glaswegians have inspired this? Glasgow was as foreign as any city I had ever seen; its strangeness was of time rather than space. It recalled certain expressionist movies set in another century, filmed in black and white to charge the screen with cheerlessness and despair. It had all the vivid unreality of artistic realism. When I later saw Thomas Annan's photographs of Glasgow's old streets, I felt that what I experienced was what he had portrayed 100 years earlier. The tenement area that he was commissioned to document before its demolition had once been praised for its orchards and gardens and pleasant odors. With astonishing speed the nineteenth century had transformed it into quite another scene, with a distinctly different odor. My first impression of Glasgow was sharp and unexpected, one that I did not experience again, although later I occasionally saw alleyways there that I am sure, if photographed, would appear virtually indistinguishable from the closes in Annan's documentation made 100 years ago.

Only seven miles southwest of Glasgow was Paisley; the two places were joined by a city bus. The space between was continuously urban, although not at all the dismal landscape that so appalled me in Glasgow. Even though I had wanted Paisley to be isolated and removed, I was not disappointed by the proximity to Glasgow, since Glasgow itself had all the dramatic isolation that I fancied for Paisley.

The Paisley Museum is in the center of town, across from the historic Paisley Abbey. The bus from Glasgow stops right there at Paisley Cross. Any tourists who happen to be in this part of Scotland are probably attracted to that ancient structure rather than to the museum. But no other outsiders were evident in either place. Greater Glasgow, which includes Paisley, was peculiarly lacking in tourists, despite the attractions of the surrounding landscape, so splendid and storied, with its Loch Lomond, the Trossachs, the Hebrides.

Young people on the streets in Paisley were extremely "mod" that year, more so than in London. At first I interpreted this as an exaggerated reaction against living in a place forever identified with old shawls. But after a brief acquaintance with the town, I concluded that the glorious past was scarcely a controlling force and that my expectations and interpretations would have seemed outrageous and confounding to the local residents.

The small museum housed natural history specimens and artifacts from the area. The textiles occupied only a small section on the second floor; they were not featured as I expected. Prominent in the exhibition was a small model of a typical weaver's cottage at the time the shawls were being woven. The label said that a special arrangement of windows indicated that this was a weaving establishment: three windows on one side of the front door. A loom would have been placed at each of the front windows, with other looms at three corresponding windows in the rear of the cottage. The building accommodated not only a six-loom shop but also living quarters on the other side of the front door. A master weaver and his family lived there, and sometimes apprentices boarded in the house. Other weavers and the drawboys (those who worked with the weavers at the drawlooms) lived elsewhere in the town and came in to work. The arrangement seemed greatly overcrowded for the small space. I learned later that this was probably relatively spacious for Paisley at the time of the shawl trade; that living, especially for the poor, became intolerable in Paisley because of the overcrowding; that dread conditions comparable to those in the worst tenements of large industrial cities—like those shown in Thomas Annan's photographs of Glasgow—prevailed in Paisley, quite contrary to one's expectations of a town in a lovely Scottish landscape. Paisley's low living standards and working conditions permitted the shawls to be turned out cheaply. Driven by famine, desperate families came from the Highlands and Ireland, attracted to the successful town, even though there was no adequate housing for them. A third of Paisley's families lived in one-room houses—and many of these rooms were cellars, small and damp, with low ceilings. Among the principal towns of Scotland, Paisley had the lowest number of rooms in proportion to the population.

I wanted to see an actual cottage, but, incomprehensibly, I could find no one who even knew whether any still remained, despite the fact that so recently a large population of weavers had worked in such cottages. With so many ancient buildings surviving in Paisley, it seemed unlikely that no weavers' cottages were still standing. Walking down the streets, I kept looking for the distinctive distribution of windows.

In the neighboring town of Kilbarchan, I saw a weaver's cottage preserved as a museum. Although it was rather similar to the model of the Paisley cottage and was probably identical to the weaving cottages that once stood in Paisley, the Kilbarchan cottage did not satisfy me. Kilbarchan chose a different path from Paisley's, even though the two towns are so close together and were subject to similar influences. Whereas Paisley specialized and finally converted its weaving to Jacquard looms and a factory system of production, Kilbarchan kept producing a wide range of woven goods on a cottage basis.

When I returned to Paisley ten years later (Glasgow was no longer so black; it was undergoing a sweeping urban renewal program), I was directed to a weaver's cottage still standing close to the museum. The poet Robert Tannahill had lived there and had worked at his loom. The cottage, built in 1776, is now a meeting place for the Paisley Burns Club. I was able to observe only from the outside. What immediately struck me was the building's small size. The space appeared entirely unrelated to what reportedly had been inside. Harness looms were huge and each required two operators: a weaver at the bench and a drawboy working beside the loom. Space was needed for movement. Yet four looms were housed in a single room. A friend who was able to visit inside the Tannahill cottage in 1976 reported that the workshop area had not been modernized as had the living quarters now occupied by caretakers. The only indications of the looms were indentations worn in the heavy grey stones by the windows where the looms had once been installed. The windows look out on what was formerly a field where horses were tethered. In the attic a loom remains, but inaccessible and unseeable since it was sealed from view by a false wall during the modernization. My friend remarked how fortunate it was that Tannahill had been a well-known Scottish poet; otherwise his weaver's cottage would not have been preserved.

Obviously, the Paisley cottages were part of the earth, enclosing, with small, deep-set openings—in a climate notorious for its grey dreariness. The ceilings were so low that, when Jacquard attachments replaced the drawboys, the space above the looms could not accommodate the new attachments.

The memoirs of David Gilmour, a man who had been a drawboy in Paisley, described his particular shop. Not only the space not occupied by looms but also "all the window sills were filled with verbenas, roses, and other flowering or sweet-scented plants, with the combined odors of which the place was saturated. The front door was kept closed, and the long garden behind, with its fruit trees, bushes, flower beds, and bee-skeps, was a really pleasant retreat. . . ."[8]

These words suggest something quite different from what is implied by the model cottage and even by the Tannahill cottage. The former is an isolated object devoid of a setting, while the latter is equally isolated amidst new streets and buildings. I suppose a ride through Britain, especially by rail, gives any traveler a feeling for dwellings related to kitchen gardens—orchards and vegetable gardens and, of course, beds of flowers. When weaving in Scotland was largely a domestic system, such a relationship must have been common, even when weaving was pursued in shops in towns and hamlets.

The Paisley weaver's cottages were quite different from the workshops of Lyon, the center of the French silk industry, which was also famous for shawls and which, directly and indirectly, exerted a powerful influence on Paisley. The Lyon weavers and their families, like those in Paisley, lived in houses scattered over the town. But in Lyon the workshops were in the upper stories of tall, narrow buildings, with the looms set before specially constructed windows to get the best possible light. The tall narrow buildings with broad windows reputedly gave Lyon a unique appearance. The studios must have seemed lifted to the light. When French weavers emigrated to England, houses were built especially for them in the East of London known as Spitalfields. The looms were on the upper floors, with long windows and space in the roof for the complicated upper works of the large drawlooms and the Jacquard mechanisms. Weavers were separated from the earth, from the gardens of vegetables and flowers that were so important to the Paisley weavers.

The model of the cottage in Paisley represented the exterior; the interior was what intrigued me. I could not envisage the spatial organization, the surroundings and conditions. I regretted that no photographs had been taken, or preserved, from the time when street scenes and buildings were photographed in nineteenth-century Paisley. Perhaps the darkness discouraged such interior photography, or perhaps this humdrum aspect of Paisley life (the activity that would make it world-famous for many years to come) seemed not worth recording. The only known photographs of the weavers and their looms show several men, wearing the typical white linen aprons tied high around their waists (Paisley weavers have been described as standing with their hands under aprons tied under their armpits), standing outside a cottage next to a dismantled loom. I fancy that the photograph represented a commonplace scene when the shawl industry was declining and when looms were being converted. The photographer seems to have unwittingly documented the historic moment when the long tradition of handweaving ended.

I worried about the light inside the cottages for such complex and fine weaving. Even when workshops had ample windows, additional light was always required because working hours were so long. When conditions grew desperate in Paisley, toward the end of the shawl trade, weaving started at six in the morning and continued until dusk during the summer months, and often until ten, eleven, or twelve during the winter. Sometimes the weavers and drawboys worked all night to earn a day off at holiday season. In drawings of the French weaving studios, candles are shown hung in contraptions around the workers' necks; other candles are suspended from racks fastened to the looms so that they shine directly on the work. The oil lamp, which is such a conspicuous feature of the paintings and drawings of weavers that Van Gogh made in nineteenth century Holland, appears quite inadequate even to light the plain cloth being woven. Paisley workshops with their infinitely complex looms must have relied on similar lamps. Books say only that Paisley weavers were required to provide their own candles and oil.

Only recently have I had a glimmering of what the Paisley weaving shops might have been like inside, but these intimations are slight and perhaps unreliable. Certainly what I first imagined is not what I imagine now. Two occurrences gave me some enlightenment. The first was reading a book published in 1871 written by David Gilmour, who had been a Paisley drawboy many years earlier and who proposed to record some of the old methods. He was the one who recalled the flowers in the window of the loom shop. The second was visiting a workshop outside Cairo where several handweavers and their assistants worked in close quarters weaving on Jacquard looms.

In describing old methods, Gilmour compared a weaving shop of looms doing plain weave with a shop of drawlooms doing fancy weaving. He personally enjoyed the "unusual stir and noise"[9] of the draw shop. He felt that the manners and general bearing of the shawl weavers were different from those of the plain weavers, as different as the goods they were producing. He recalled when Paisley was one huge weaving factory of master weavers upon whom the well-being and comfort of the whole population depended. Weavers had a sense of their own significance, which undoubtedly fostered a kind of conduct and attitude reflected in the tone of the workshops.

In reading Gilmour's account I was struck, as much as anything, by a few details he happened to mention (I regretted that he had not included more, now lost forever). He said that the drawboys worked barefoot during the summer, and that there was singing in the weaving shops. The weavers and drawboys sang together as they worked. At other times they listened to one of the group. They derived solace, Gilmour said, from singing. The boys were obliged to have the looms dusted, the spindles oiled, and other chores accomplished before the master's arrival in the morning. If anything were amiss, the boys received rough treatment when the weavers arrived: cuffs and kicks and even horsewhipping. Gilmour said that what never failed to astonish him after such rough disciplining was that "long before breakfast hour the master and boy were singing some favorite song together."[10]

I recalled the bus ride I had taken into the Highlands on a day's outing, the weather being suddenly brilliant. The other passengers were Scots who didn't know each other and they didn't talk together even when we stopped for tea; but they all sang together. They sang all the way home, one song after another, in full, unhesitant voices. The driver sang solos and then the passengers joined in. And then a passenger sang solo, quite without embarrassment. A tradition of singing had persisted, which to me was completely foreign. I had trouble accepting the direct, uncontrived outpouring; I could relate to it only in terms of an artificial Hollywood movie. I suspected that life patterns in Western Europe before the industrial revolution are already unimagineable, that a time so recent can never be accurately reconstructed.

Gilmour was not saying that a drawboy's life in a Paisley weaving shop was one of contentment—quite the contrary. The "solace" that he derived from singing was desperately needed. His decision to become a drawboy was, as he said, a very terrible mistake. Those who endured the drudgery and harsh treatment common to drawboys would certainly not sigh for the return of the "good old days."

The drawboys, who were sometimes girls and were often the children of immigrants, were under fifteen or sixteen years old, sometimes only six years old (the law that prevented the hiring of children under ten years old was not passed in Scotland until 1878). They worked hard and for long hours. A relief from the drudgery, although this was not regarded by the boys as a pleasant diversion, was the reading of the New Testament, which was often required by the parents as part of the agreement when the boys were hired.

The Saturday afternoons, which were said to be their own, were spent preparing for the work of the coming week. That was the time to sweep under the looms, under the treadles "where lodged rotten dressing, damp ravellings, spider webs, snails, and other abominations."[11] The boys washed brushes and mended broken parts, and finally were sent to the mistress for their wages.

Paisley was filled with thousands of these young boys who, when freed from the hard monotonous work, ran wild in the streets. They were a terror to everyone with their recklessness, fighting, games and mischief. They were described as rude, loud, cruel to the weak and defenseless. Many ran off to sea or escaped in other ways. The picture Matthew Blair depicts is less grim: The drawboys are a brave, cheery race, full of fun and mischief.

In the Cairo handweaving shop I saw looms filling the interior from floor to ceiling and from wall to wall. The looms thrust out in all directions, without well-defined spaces, as might appear in a model. Each loom encroached upon the next until the separate looms seemed components in some larger fantasy structure. Warps were stretched backward, upward, downward, in unpredictable configurations. The Paisley looms were perhaps more distinguishable as individual units, yet the congestion must have been about the same, as were the personal involvement and conversational exchanges, the interactions of the weavers and their assistants.

What was immediately apparent from the model of the Paisley cottage was that the weavers were not working in isolation, but neither were they in what we now think of as factories. It occurred to me (later I realized that I had once read something similar in a book about the shawls) that this small group situation may well have stimulated the technical innovations that characterized Paisley looms, just as it fostered an independence of thought and a radicalism among Paisley weavers. Small groups of weavers were in constant contact with each other discussing and arguing while they worked at their looms that were crowded together in small spaces. While Tannahill worked at his loom, he kept a notebook at his side to jot down ideas for poetry. Other Paisley weavers are reported to have had inkbottles near at hand to jot down bits of verse or arguments as they worked. The early shawl weavers were known for their literacy and for their libraries. They were aware of each other's work, solutions, and innovations. Weavers ate their meals together (even their breakfasts) and afterwards gathered around the fire to smoke and talk. Often, each weaver in a cottage contributed a small amount to pay for a newspaper subscription; the paper was passed from weaver to weaver and the news was discussed. Four o'clock in the afternoon, when the loom was at the "close-mou'," was a regular time to smoke pipes and lounge in the doorway if the day happened to be sunny. (In the weaving process, the warp yarns, which are stretched on the loom, are "opened" to accept the weft, or filler, yarns; when the loom is at rest, this opening, called the shed, is closed. In Paisley the loom at rest was called the "close-mouth." Describing the shed as a mouth creates an unforgettable image of the loom as something alive, constantly consuming, voracious and insatiable.) When they no longer wove in cottages but worked in factories where they were poorly paid, the weavers were less radical politically.

While it is comfortable to envisage Paisley at the time of the shawl manufacture as a town of little streets lined with six-loom shops with additional cottages in the surrounding area for the weavers and drawboys who did not live in the shops, the scene was considerably more varied. During the peak years, Paisley had 7,000 weavers, mostly shawl weavers. Of these, many owned their own looms, which were installed in their own homes or their own small shops. Others who owned their own looms rented a "stance" or working space in a loom shop. Many weavers did not own their own looms—they could not afford to buy them (the looms for fancy weaving were considerably more expensive than looms for plain weaving) so they hired the use of looms in order to do their work. Sometimes a weaver who wove on someone else's loom received a percentage of what his weaving earned. Among harness weavers—which included shawl weavers—half did not own their own looms but paid for the use of a loom with a quarter of their earnings. Other weavers were employees who received wages for working in shops.

A manufacturer supplied the "web," the amount of yarn for weaving a piece of cloth. The weaver provided the light and fire, and the starch for dressing the warp. (The application of a starch dressing to the fine warp yarns strengthened them, enabling them to withstand the friction and tension of weaving.) The weaver picked up the web from the manufacturer and, when it was woven, returned it to the warehouse where he was paid. Weavers who did not live close to a manufactory were served by agents who worked on a commission basis—supplying the webs, etc.

Even though they could have earned more money working away from home, many weavers preferred not to work in a shop or a factory, where the loom and web were provided by the manufacturer and the warp was wound onto the loom by machinery. While handweavers could have earned more by going into the spinning or power loom factories, they preferred not to identify themselves with the immigrant class that accepted such work. More than higher wages, the weaver valued his independence and "image of himself as a craftsman."[12]

Until 1840 the shawl trade was predominantly a home industry. The weaver working at home was his own master; he set his own hours and came and went at his own convenience. After all, a long tradition existed for combining weaving with agricultural duties, so that weaving had for many years been a part-time activity to be done when it was not convenient to work outdoors. Weavers enjoyed being able to respond to the weather or the season, taking a day's pleasure to go fishing or berrying. They could make up the work at some other time. A shawl was a long project, sometimes worked at for six months; the time could be adjusted. According to statistics for piecework in the British cotton weaving industry, the handloom weaver was satisfied with the "conventionally comfortable standard of living" which "the old desultory habits of work provided."[13] This attitude was probably characteristic of Paisley weavers early in the shawl industry. They did not force themselves to produce more and more but were content with a modest income, setting themselves flexible schedules that were not too tedious and allowed time for pleasures. Later on, this easy-going quality disappeared.

This is a rare photograph of a Paisley loom. The Jacquard attachment is crowded against the ceiling. The punched cards can be seen at left center. The fly-shuttle is evident below the cards. The loom that produced such refined and complex weaving was a rough, clumsy-looking affair. The photograph was taken in Charleston, a village that grew outside the town of Paisley and became part of the textile center. (Courtesy: Paisley Museum and Art Galleries)

When the power loom was being introduced (not for shawl weaving; nevertheless the power loom profoundly, although indirectly, influenced shawl weavers) many weavers opposed the new work since the power looms were necessarily installed at the source of power and therefore required the weavers to come to the looms. Similar changes occurred when the Jacquards were used for shawl weaving. Weavers could no longer afford to own their looms. Furthermore, the cottages could not accommodate the new mechanisms because of the height and weight. Manufacturers or entrepreneurs owned the Jacquards, which were installed—from fifteen to fifty—in factories where the weavers were obliged to work and often to live with their families in woeful tenement conditions. In the earlier domestic situation, the entire family helped with preparing the fiber for spinning, as well as with the spinning and dyeing. The family then wound the yarn onto bobbins for the shuttles used by the weaver. When the weaving was completed, the family knotted the fringes and did the necessary finishing. In some cases the women were able to do the actual weaving, although this was considered to be man's work. When workers were obliged to relate their lives to the power looms and the Jacquards in factories, these family patterns broke down. As weaving became drudgery, Paisley weavers became known for taking comfort in drink and filling the town with drunken brawling.

In a book written at the time when the shawl industry was declining in Paisley, William Jolly spoke of the earlier days when

> Weavers then formed as a whole, a remarkable class of men—intelligent and observant of the progress of events at home and abroad; devoted to politics, strongly or wildly radical, if not tainted with revolutionary sentiments after the intoxication of the first French Revolution; great talkers when they gathered in the streets or public-house, during the intervals of work; . . . general guardians of the Church, reformers of the state, and proud patrons of learning and the schoolmaster; but, withal, good fathers, good churchmen, good citizens, and not seldom good men.[14]

In twenty years weavers had degenerated from poverty and excessive toil, to men with neither "leisure, aptitude, nor desire for information."[15]

(Left) In 1978, Tannahill's cottage shows a beautiful, decorative thatch roof. Adjoining buildings have been replaced by a garden and walks. The sensation is of massive masonry enclosing.

4. The Looms
The problem of handwoven vs machinewoven

It is interesting to speculate about the time late in the eighteenth century when Cashmeres became fashionable, when European weavers first studied the shawls to find ways to copy them using mechanical looms.

The qualities of Cashmeres that first appealed to Europeans were the softness, lightness, smoothness, and the sinuous drape. These—the texture and handle—derived largely from the fiber, although also from the weave. In imitating the shawls Europeans tried to obtain the fiber and even to raise the animals that produced it. These efforts have been described by John Irwin in his

(Opposite, bottom) Shawl weavers at Srinager, Kashmir. Two weavers work side by side at a relatively narrow strip of twill-tapestry weaving. They use a simple horizontal loom. The four shafts or harnesses required by the twill are evident. (Courtesy: The American Museum of Natural History)

Fig. 1ere

59

(Above) Tapestry weaving on a vertical loom in France, as illustrated in Diderot's Encyclopedia. The weaving does not progress uniformly from selvage to selvage but builds up in certain areas where the weaver chooses to concentrate his energies for a while. The twill-tapestry of Cashmere shawls built up row by row, from selvage to selvage. This difference in technique is of utmost significance in the appearance of tapestry. The bobbins of weft are shown hanging out of the way, whereas in Cashmere tapestry weaving, the bobbins lay on the completed work. In France, the weaving was beaten down with a small comb; in Kashmir, the reed of the loom beat the weft, creating regular horizontal lines of weaving rather than the irregularities of European tapestries. The cartoon can be seen behind the stretched warps. For shawls, a different method was used in following preplanned patterns: in Scotland specialists worked away from the loom translating the drawings into symbols from which the looms were programmed; in India instructions were read to the weavers. (Reproduced courtesy of The Bancroft Library, University of California, Berkeley)

two books on shawls (see Bibliography). A single episode characterizes all the ill-fated ventures: with great difficulty a starter herd of the rare goats was obtained for transport from Central Asia to England. To avoid difficulties in transit, the males and females were sent in separate ships. Alas, one of the two ships sank in a storm.

When they were unable to obtain the Cashmere fiber, Europeans settled for a combination of fibers with which they were well acquainted. Silk and wool were skillfully blended to form fine strong yarn for warps and for those wefts not creating the pattern. Sometimes silk alone was used. Heavier worsted yarns were used for the pattern wefts.

In Cashmere shawls the glossy fiber was shown off by the twill weave. The wefts moved over two warps then under two warps in what is called a 2/2 twill. The diagonal movement throughout the shawls was a visually prominent feature. This was easy for Europeans to copy. Throughout all the years of production of Paisley-type shawls, the twill, or semblance of the twill, appeared even when the shawls were imitated by printing.

Because the wefts were not beaten down hard, the warps of Cashmere shawls showed in the finished textiles. This beating made a soft, flexible fabric and, in addition, permitted the warp color to show slightly (a red warp gave a slight redness throughout the patterns and background). Europeans took great pains to imitate this feature.

The Cashmere patterns were woven in a tapestry technique, although not exactly the same technique as traditional European tapestries. European tapestries were plain weave (over one, under one), beaten down hard to cover the warps and make the textiles thick and substantial, often quite architectural. The Cashmeres were 2/2 twill, more open, allowing the cloth to be flexible.

Paisley weavers were familiar with twill-tapestry and they were sufficiently skilled to weave shawls using this technique. The problem was that tapestry was painfully slow at a time when goods for the fashion market had to be turned out fast and when goods for the new mass market had to be cheap. Furthermore, the thrust in European textiles was toward the mechanical. Europeans had to find faster solutions to ancient problems. How else could they compete with workers throughout the world whose standards of living were so low?

Tapestry is the technical antithesis of mechanical weaving. In nineteenth century Europe, tapestry was recognized as a technique that could not be adapted to mechanical looms and could not be powerwoven. This endeared tapestry to the English designer William Morris, who learned to weave tapestry and was active in reviving tapestry weaving. He described tapestry, in which there is nothing mechanical, as the noblest of the weaving arts.[16] At about the same time, the textile technician E. A. Posselt said that tapestry is neither real weaving nor true embroidering. "Though wrought upon a loom and upon a warp stretched out along its frame, there is no filling thrown across the threads with a shuttle. . . ."[17] He regarded tapestry work to be the most costly of the textile manufacture. He also considered it to be the most effective. How Europeans imitated the tapestry patterns will be discussed later.

The Cashmeres were not like European tapestries, which imitated paintings, but, rather, they were straightforward woven constructions, formed obviously by a systematic intersection of yarns at right angles. Tiny shapes of different colors fit together to create rather geometric flowers and leaves. Many tiny parallelograms appeared compactly arranged. The Europeans described this as a mosaic effect and imitated it in their shawls. The angular, broken and nervous tipped contours of Cashmere patterns were maintained in the European shawls, whether woven or printed.

Important to the appearance of certain Cashmere patterning was the fact that some of the shawls were not single pieces of weaving but were composed of separate woven pieces assembled into a single shawl. The assembling was done skillfully enough to be virtually imperceptible. Many Cashmeres were bordered in multicolored patches sewed together, appearing as a single piece of weaving. Since each patch was woven on a separate warp (the work could be parcelled out to various weavers and various looms, production time being thereby reduced), one patch might have a blue warp, the next patch a red warp, etc. The colors of these various warps showed in the fringe and also in the color imparted to the weaving. Paisley-type shawls ingeniously imitated the unusual effect without resorting to assembling separate pieces.

To speed the production of the central areas of their shawls, Kashmir workers assembled shaped pieces of woven and embroidered patterns. The results were dramatic contrasts of light and dark patches, assembled freely like collages. Paisley-type shawls imitated the appearance of many irregular-shaped patchworks of pattern but never really captured the collage quality.

A feature of all tapestries is that the yarns that create the patterns are the same yarns that construct the cloth. This is described as structure creating pattern. To a non-weaver this may not seem remarkable; to a weaver it is a significant distinction, separating tapestry from the many woven patterns created by yarns that are an addition to the structural yarns. In tapestry no yarns are excess; to remove a yarn from warp or weft destroys the fabric. Since the pattern *is* the cloth, it never appears applied. Structural patterning gives a

62   special look to a textile. More than that, its concept is intellectually appealing. Paisley-type shawls tried to achieve the appearance of structural weaving.

Brocade was tried as a logical substitute for tapestry, but it was slow and it appeared applied, not structural. Another technique had to be found. The solution was a technique that allowed weft yarns to float outside the weaving. These floats were later cut off, leaving only the woven portions. In the finished shawl, the pattern wefts were no longer continuous yarns from selvage to selvage but were short snatches of yarns, each woven securely where the color was required by the pattern. The fabric was held together by other wefts. The technique is described as a kind of extra-weft patterning. It is also described as discontinuous weft patterning.

Fragment of a Paisley-type shawl shown in exact size.

The back of the Paisley-type fragment shown in exact size.

Enlarged detail of the fragment.

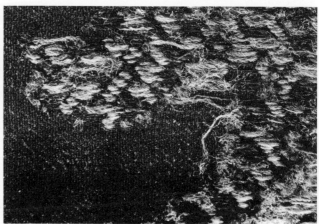

Enlarged detail of the back of the fragment.

Paisley-type shawl with large brocaded motives, each about fourteen inches high, in yellow, red, white and blue, against a black silk background. On the back side, nothing is clipped. (Collection: Robert H. Lowie Museum of Anthropology, University of California, Berkeley)

Back of shawl. Separate borders have been attached. The shawl is heavy with the weight of the yarns required to brocade the pattern. (Collection: Robert H. Lowie Museum of Anthropology, University of California, Berkeley)

For various reasons, weavers throughout history have imitated the appearance of one textile technique by using another technique. The great Gothic tapestries used tapestry to imitate the appearance of silk patterns, just as Paisley weavers used extra-weft techniques to imitate the appearance of tapestries. Each weaving technique has its own potential for color distribution and pattern shapes. When one weaving technique imitates another, the medium is forced, effects are contrived, and wonderful surprises result. When the Paisley extra-weft technique imitated tapestry patterns, the result was a flood of superfluous, unattached weft pouring from the back of the weaving. Actually, the weaver faced the superfluous yarns; these are what he saw as he wove, since the back of the shawl was up. The floating yarns completely obscured the developing pattern. After the weaving was removed, all these floats had to be cut away. They left a velvety surface of surpassing visual beauty and delightful tactile texture—one of the special qualities of Paisley-type shawls. They had the beauty of pile fabric with the rich texture and color of many cut ends of fine yarns. The velutinous backs tend to make Paisley-type shawls easily distinguishable from Cashmeres.

During the weaving process, the pattern wefts went from one selvage to the other. This was important for fast weaving and minimum hand manipulation. In its route across, the pattern shuttle entered the warp only where its color was required by the pattern; everywhere else it floated free. To make the woven portions continuous across a pattern row, several shuttles were required, each carrying its own color and each entering the weaving as called for by the pattern. These shuttles were thrown across in regular sequence, always in the same color order. When the sequence was complete—when a row of weft pattern was woven—the opening was changed and one or more structural weft yarns was entered from selvage to selvage to keep the pattern yarns firmly in place. These structural wefts were very fine—usually either silk or cotton.

The Cashmere tapestry patterns allowed any number of colors to appear anywhere in the textile. Paisley designers were limited in their colors by the number of shuttles the loom could accommodate (the shuttles had to fit into special slots, called "lay boxes," attached at each side of the loom; only a limited number of such slots were feasible). By adroit use of the limited number of shuttles, designers achieved the dense multicolor effects of tapestry with shuttles that moved from one selvage to the other as required for fast mechanical patterning. Like the Cashmere tapestries, the Paisley-type shawls avoided an appearance of color in horizontal bands.

The technique gave patterns with all threads well held down, front and back. Although the patterns consisted entirely of short bits of yarn, they did not unravel. The snatches of yarn were remarkably secure because they were held in a warp that was fine and dense, and because the pattern wefts were wool and were always followed by a structural weft. The textiles required no linings since there were no floats to snag. And the shawls could be woven relatively quickly by one weaver and his drawboy.

Shawls woven in this extra-weft technique are unusually flat and regular. No areas of crowded wefts make the surface variable, and no interlocking of wefts creates slight ridges at the joinings. The regularity of the Paisley-type surface gives a tactile quality quite unlike that of a Cashmere, although the two kinds of shawl appear amazingly similar. Paisley patterns emerge with remarkable precision, emphasized by the smooth refined yarns of warp and weft. The technique and the yarns, together with the great skill of the weavers, foster the mechanical look so often attributed to Paisleys.

That this mechanical look was distasteful to the Europeans is quite unlikely. They found enormous satisfaction in machines and their marvelous, abundant accomplishments. In a sense, the mechanical perfection was the fulfillment of a long search in textile production, not only in Europe. While the Indians regretted the decline in taste due to European influence (just as they had regretted the changes in their brocades and painted cottons), the Europeans felt that the shawl designs were improved by their influence. The designs, which were inspired by the mechanical looms, were admired for the elaborations, the intricacy of compositions. Such complexity of color and pattern were new and remarkable in woven designs.

1. Detail, Paisley-type woven shawl. The shearing or shaving of the excess weft yarns on the back was a critical operation, the work of specialists. Early in the industry, the job took a woman an entire day to clip the floats from a single shawl. When the weaving came from the loom, a shawl might weigh 100 ounces; after shearing it weighed 34 ounces, the average weight of a good quality plaid. Later, shearing machines, rather like lawn mowers, with revolving blades, were introduced from France. Shawls were called ''covered work,'' possibly because the weft floats covered the pattern as the weaver worked. (Collection: Katherine Westphal)

2. *Detail, printed Paisley-type shawl. Even though the cloth is lightweight wool challis, the dye penetrates unevenly, giving the shawl only one good side. The garment is lightweight and drapes beautifully while showing elaborate patterns and colors. Such printed shawls carefully imitated the appearance of the woven shawls; other printed shawls used the design motives without imitating weaving. (Collection: Pat Hickman)*

3. *Detail Cashmere patchwork shawl composed of woven pieces and embroidered pieces. On the back, the wefts can be seen moving diagonally from place to place as required by the pattern. Sometimes two Cashmere shawls were worn back to back to conceal the tangle of yarns. The backs of Paisley-type shawls appear different because the ends of the yarn are clipped and always move horizontally. Today the floating and clipped wefts of Cashmeres and Paisleys are considered to be appealing features. (Collection: Pat Charley)*

4. *Fashionable wear for churchgoing. Shawls kept increasing in size along with the costumes so that shawls, even when doubled over, reached from the shoulders to the floor. When the bustle became stylish, the special fashionable part of the costume was concealed by the shawl. This unfortunate circumstance is sometimes blamed for ending the rage of shawls. From* Le Journal des Dames et des Demoiselles, *March 1857 (Reproduced by courtesy of Dan Reserva, Munich, in Ciba-Geigy Journal, N2-73 Summer)*

5. Detail, Paisley-type woven plaid shawl. Many late shawls became large compositions of abstract motives, boldly emblematic, in which the multitude of tiny mosaic-like flowers filling all the divisions became secondary, scarcely recognizable. (Collection: Katherine Westphal)

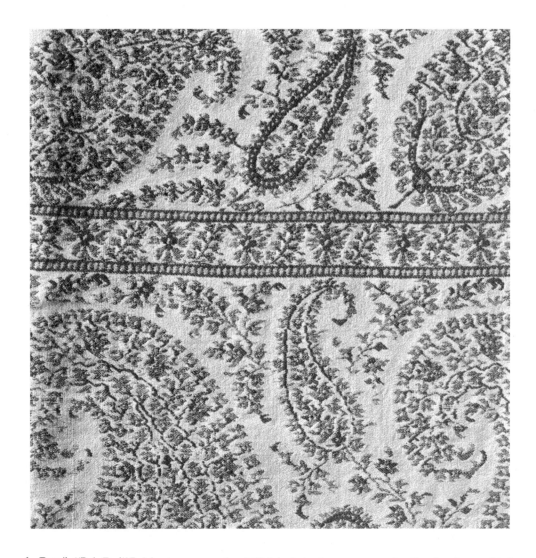

6. *Detail, "Pale End" Paisley-type woven shawl. This imitates the appearance of earlier shawls assembled from separate borders and end panels. (Collection: Program in Visual Design, University of California, Berkeley)*

7. *Printed wool shawl imitating a late Jacquard-woven shawl inspired by a patchwork Cashmere. The five-foot square is outlined with printed rectangles that suggest separate patches. The color of each "patch" extends into the fringe to simulate the warp fringes of woven tabs. The irregular white lines that move so dramatically through the dense patterning recall the startling value contrasts achieved in Cashmere patchwork. The printing imitates even the joining of separate tabs in Cashmeres. Because woven Paisleys are so diagrammatic, so mechanical, they are easily imitated by printing. From a photograph it is impossible to distinguish a woven shawl from a printed imitation. (Collection: Pat Hickman)*

8. Detail, printed Paisley-type shawl. Many blocks are carefully registered to produce precise, clear patterns. Printed shawls that imitate the woven variety seem to return the designs to their appearance in working drawings and sketches—diagrammatic and specific, without the softening that occurs in the weaving process. (Collection: Pat Hickman)

9. Pages from a dye book with swatches of printed cloth showing Paisley motives. The dye book, from the eighteenth and nineteenth centuries, was used by the eldest son of John Peel, a dyer of Lancashire, England. (Collection: Program in Visual Design, University of California, Berkeley)

10. Printed Paisley shawl. The precision of the printing and the clarity of the dye colors invited the sharply defined corner treatment with a diagonal motive added to avoid any irregular meeting of the block. (Collection: Paisley Museum and Art Galleries)

11. *(Right) Sketch of motives for Paisley shawls. Specifications for the threading often appear alongside the sketches. (Collection: Paisley Museum and Art Galleries)*

12. *(Below) Paisley patterns for sprigs, about 1838. Sprig motives were adapted from the decorative arts of the Near East, India and China. Pages of these motives were prepared for use in various ways by shawl designers. Some of the sprigs in this illustration show the influence of Chinese cloud motives. (Collection: Paisley Museum and Art Galleries)*

13. *Sketch for a portion of a Paisley shawl, 1828–36. It carries the name Thomas Baird & Son, Causeyside. (Collection: Paisley Museum and Art Galleries)*

14. *Trial prints of a complex block for a printed Paisley shawl, 1854. On the left is the print on paper with pencilled notations; overlapping it on the right is the print on cloth. The manufacturer was Forbes & Hutchinson, Forbes Place. (Collection: Paisley Museum and Art Galleries)*

15. *Black-center Paisley-type woven shawl. When the drafted and painted designs were rendered in yarn on the loom, the color shapes lost some of their mosaic-like precision. Colors in small bits intermingled and interacted—not unlike the color used by the Impressionist painters late in the nineteenth century. The shawls glowed with the full color of dyed silk and wool, draped to create highlights and shadows. (Collection: Pat Charley)*

16. *Detail, Paisley-type woven shawl emphasizing the complementary colors red and green, and blue and orange. Paisleys often juxtaposed complements in such small color shapes that they merged into greyed texture. (Collection: Katherine Westphal)*

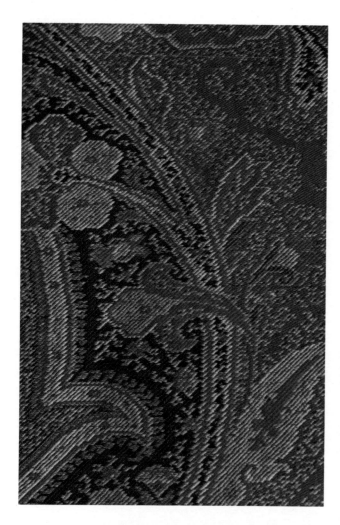

17. Detail, Paisley-type woven shawl. Paisleys were limited in the
number of shuttles that the looms could accommodate and,
therefore, in the number of weft colors that could be used. Paisleys
did not compensate by using variegated yarns or colors plied
together, or two weft colors on the same shuttle—devices that other
weavings have used to increase the color variations without
increasing the number of shuttles. Paisleys concentrated on subtle
distribution of a limited number of colors. Here, tiny bits of yellow
flicker in the red background; whites show a pinky glow; petals of
the flower use tiny bits of red in yellow shapes, and tiny bits of
yellow in red shapes to vary the color sensation. The red warp
shows throughout all the colors, modifying and unifying.
(Collection: Program in Visual Design, University of California,
Berkeley)

18. Paisley-type neck scarf. A single motive woven in the typical
technique appears at each end of the five-inch wide scarf. The
sides are cut as though a number of shawls had been woven
simultaneously and then cut apart in strips. (Collection: Program
in Visual Design, University of California, Berkeley)

19. *Paisley-type woven shawl composed of separate components. While many shawls were enormous, others were of manageable size. This one, called a stole shawl, is about ten feet long but only sixteen inches wide. (Collection: Pat Hickman)*

20. (Right) Detail, Paisley-type red-center woven shawl. The formal border, dense in both patterning and woven structure, dissolves into open, freely spaced foliage reaching into the plain center. The Paisley technique allowed many small color shapes to appear on a remarkably flat woven surface. Patterns seem to penetrate the fabric—to be the fabric. The unusual flatness of the patterned surface accounts somewhat for the shawls' machine-like look. (Collection: Maureen Irle Toftner)

21. (Below) Fragment, Paisley-type woven shawl. When shawls were reassembled or patched to save the good parts, the leftover remnants, each with its own chance imagery, were too beautiful to throw away. Like so many ancient fragments, the bits of Paisleys, preserved and treasured, were self-sufficient expressions, each with its own message.

It seems worth commenting that, until the collapse of the shawl industry, expensive Cashmere shawls continued to be woven in India in the twill-tapestry technique, but following the latest designs from Europe. These designs were more appropriate to mechanical loom weaving than to tapestry. Yet when painstakingly woven in fine material, the Cashmeres resulting from these designs were breathtaking. Each shawl was a *tour de force* that today evokes our greatest admiration. Possibly because the designs did not grow directly from the weaving technique and were not truly appropriate to the technique, the medium was stretched. When compared with these Cashmeres, similar shawls, woven in Europe on the mechanism for which they were designed, appear mechanical; yet they are free of certain nagging questions aroused by the Cashmeres, which were woven without mechanical assistance. How could so many painfully laborious Cashmere shawls have been woven? Museums and private collections are filled with them. How could Europeans have demanded this of the Asians? To see so many mechanical-looking Paisleys is not nearly so disturbing. Since weavers of India were well acquainted with drawlooms and were highly skilled in their operation, why did they not turn to drawlooms to compete with the European drawloom shawls? The Cashmeres remain as awesome accomplishments of the human hand, forever expressing Europe's enchantment with its new machines and India's desperate, feverish will to compete using its ancient hand methods. The consequences of mechanization were so pervasive, and so unpredictable.

Paisleys arouse questions of their own. Anyone versed in textile technology must be dazzled by Paisley shawls, but puzzled. Because it has been established that Paisley shawls were increasingly directed toward the middle-class mass market, the question arises: Was the public so thoroughly acquainted with the refinements of Cashmere shawls that the various aspects had to be imitated quite so slavishly? Few consumers could have recognized or demanded the extreme refinements. While high technical standards are evident in the work, so are animating aesthetic considerations seldom associated with the drive toward mechanization. There is about the Paisley-type shawls an unmistakable and surprising sense of quality of workmanship, of infinite details, of pains taken to achieve results too esoteric for a mass market to notice or value. The mass market seemed to have been either greatly respected or entirely ignored. Producers of the shawls were artists and engineers, solving aesthetic and mechanical problems that they found challenging and that they set for themselves in a time of innovation and investigation and change. In an unexpected way, they seem to have been satisfying themselves.

The question "Was it handwoven" is always asked about a Paisley. Perhaps this is an idiosyncrasy of the time so immediately following the demise of industrial handweaving. Or perhaps it occurs because Paisleys are so associated with the time when this type of handweaving died. Even when these shawls are seen only as a folded edge in a museum drawer they can recall not only Queen Victoria, Dickens, the American Civil War, and pioneering in the United States, but also industrial development and revolutionary change. So the question keeps recurring, was it handwoven?

Paisley-type shawls scarcely fit today's notions of handweaving. The patterns are too complex, the yarns too fine, and the weaving too uniform. In short, they are too machine-like. Yet museums are filled with handwoven textiles similarly complex and uniformly woven of fine yarns, which seldom invite the question since these textiles were made on mechanical looms long before the invention of power equipment. When occasionally the question is asked about such textiles, it is asked compulsively, as though against all reason; because the textiles appear so mechanical, so perfect, no one can imagine that they were *really* handwoven. Today, anything that is powerwoven, or that appears powerwoven, is instantly regarded as less interesting, expressive and beautiful, less remarkable and valuable. As the handwoven and the power-woven began to be perceived as two quite separate products, the powerwoven gradually became classified as "industrial textiles"; this effectively set them apart from all other textiles woven throughout history. The division is especially mischievous since the flow of ideas throughout textile history is continuous; the quest has so often been to achieve the uniformity, precision, repetition and fineness that reached expression in textiles classified as industrial, but these are now excluded from consideration as art.

Paradoxically, at the same time that Paisleys have been called mere mechanical weavings, they have been lauded as the epitome of handloom weaving, the peak of perfection in the development of woven fabric in color, design and weaving technique. It is difficult to say how they should be classified, not because the method of weaving is unknown today but because there is no agreement about the basis for dividing goods. A handwoven textile cannot be defined simply as one woven by hand and a powerwoven textile as one woven on a powerloom. Between the obviously handwoven and the obviously powerwoven is a great uncertain area.

For a long time Europe's fancy textiles were without question handwoven. Such textiles were fabricated on specialized mechanical equipment by expert weavers and designers able to devote time to the work. As social conditions in Europe changed, more people aspired to own fancy goods, but, at the same time, they demanded greater quantities of everyday textiles. One by one, improvements in textile production were introduced into Europe: the fly-shuttle, the Jacquard attachment, the spinning mule, the powerloom. The intention was not to produce new kinds of textiles but to produce the familiar ones faster, using less human energy. When powerlooms were invented, goods were made as identical as possible to the handwoven; often the two could not be told apart. Because the powerwoven cloth was more even than the handwoven, the powerwoven became so popular that "powerloom" was sometimes stamped on handwoven cloth by dishonest merchants.

The industrial revolution's Textile Phase, which extended from 1780 to 1840, was concerned with waterpower and steampower for spinning and weaving cotton. When it ended, most textiles were still being woven by hand. The number of handlooms in England and Scotland was still enormous—four times that of powerlooms. But the way had been prepared for unbelievably rapid changes during the next ten years.

The Textile Phase saw the town of Paisley turning from the weaving of fancy cotton muslins and silk gauzes to shawls. The fancy goods, which gave Paisley its reputation, could not yet be woven by the new powerlooms. Yet change was in the air, threatening and influencing. Paisley weavers derived hope from the belief that the "skilled departments of handweaving" were exempt from the danger; that power could be applied only to the lower branches of handweaving. Even so, the fancy weavers were feeling the effects of the powerlooms since these new inventions were producing cheap cotton cloths as alternatives to the handwoven silks and linens, which were truly victims of the powerloom. Furthermore, competition from the powerloom was driving handweavers out of the plain trade into the fancy trade, until the supply of handweavers was far exceeding the demand.

While these changes were occurring, Paisley handweavers kept modifying the old handlooms. Looking back now, it seems that the mechanical improvements that they devised were, in truth, part of the movement toward the final dreaded "improvement." The dilemma was that the weavers' survival lay in the cultivation of their mechanical ingenuity if they were to compete successfully with the world's handweavers, and that mechanical improvements led irresistably to the powerloom.

The Paisley handcraftsmen seem to have established boundaries to how much mechanization was acceptable. As long as possible, they resisted installation of the Jacquard attachment that was being used so successfully by handweavers in France in the production of shawls. The Paisley weavers considered the Jacquard *too* mechanical. For them it was more than a mechanization of the drawloom; it was the end of a way of life. For although the Jacquard was not a powerloom (it began as a hand-operated attachment installed on a conventional loom), it meant that the weaver became a factory worker because Jacquards were so expensive, high and heavy that they could not be cottage equipment.

In 1833, there were only thirty-six Jacquard looms in Scotland; they were all in Paisley, in one factory. At that time there were more than 5,000 drawboys in Paisley. But in the years following 1840, when the powerlooms were triumphing over the handlooms in Britain, the Jacquard triumphed over the old drawloom in Paisley. (To my great disappointment, the shawl loom on exhibit in the Paisley Museum turned out to be a Jacquard rather than the early drawloom I was so anxious to see.) The Jacquard could no longer be resisted since it increased the potential for weaving the large complex designs with elaborate details and flowing lines that were becoming fashionable. It also increased production in a number of ways apart from the speed and convenience with which Jacquards could be converted to weave new designs. Handweavers working in factories produced more than handweavers working at home. The factory situation permitted a greater specialization among the workers. Also, the weavers could be forced to work longer hours since the Jacquard dispensed with the drawboys, who were unable to endure the long hours required of adults (plain weavers working on simple looms, which they could operate without assistance, put in fourteen or fifteen hours a day; whereas the harness weavers working on drawlooms, which required the constant help of an assistant, or drawboy, worked only twelve hours a day).

Paisley had a variety of looms, appropriate to the goods being woven. Many of the drawlooms on which the early shawls were woven were equipped with, as the British would say, two harnesses; they were double harness looms. The word *harness* is confusing since its meaning in the United States is not the same as it is in Britain. In the United States a harness is a single shaft; a four-harness loom has four shafts. In Britain a harness is an entire system of shafts. So that the Paisley drawlooms, with two harnesses, had two entire systems of shafts mounted on one loom. (The double harness loom is not to be confused with what, in the United States, was often used in weaving coverlets and is called a multiple harness handloom. Such a loom has numerous shafts, sometimes as many as twenty-four or more all comprising one harness in the British sense. Although many patterns were possible with the multiple harness loom, more intricate patterns required the drawloom.) The weaving from the Paisley looms with their double harnesses was called harness weaving; the shawls were called harness shawls; the looms were called harness looms.

In the Paisley drawlooms with their double harness systems, each warp was threaded through both harnesses. The conventional harness with four to eight shafts was called the ground harness or binder harness. It was used to make openings for the wefts that were not creating the patterns. It was

Since sets of Jacquard cards were expensive to prepare, cards for the previous year's patterns were later used for weaving shawls in cheaper materials and for lower prices. Toward the end of the industry, this corruption of the designs contributed to the shawls' poor reputation and their demise.

Returning to the question of whether Paisleys were handwoven, it can be said that Paisley shawls were woven by handweavers using mechanical looms. All looms are machines, which, by definition, are "structures consisting of a framework and various fixed and moving parts for doing some kind of work."[19] The looms in Kashmir were frameworks with few moving parts; the looms in Paisley were frameworks with many moving parts, and they were of such bewildering complexity that they are called mechanical. Looms are sometimes divided into those that are manual and those that are mechanical; yet all looms are mechanical, the difference is in the degree.

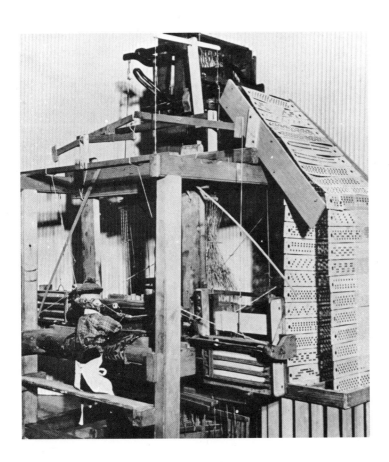

Model of Jacquard attachment on a Paisley shawl loom, about 1840. Shawls could be five feet wide and twelve feet long, using eight to ten different wefts. The cards laced together were called a "chain." Each card in turn controlled every thread of a warp, instructing it to raise or remain in position. (Courtesy: Paisley Museum and Art Galleries)

4.—PIERCING THE CARDS FOR THE PATTERN.

Illustration from The Ladies' Treasury, *1857, showing the "piercing of the cards" for Jacquard silk weaving. The design was "read" by the assistant at the left, where determinations were made regarding the distribution of the holes. Small establishments could punch cards between two steel plates, preparing from 100 to 150 cards in a day. Large establishments could afford cardcutting machines such as the one illustrated. With this machine and the help of an assistant, a cardcutter could punch from 2500 to 3000 cards in a day. A single machine was able to supply cards for 300 looms. If more than one set of cards was wanted, the cardcutter could punch two cards at the same time if the cardboard was thin. If it was thick, one card was cut after another. (Crown copyright: Victoria & Albert Museum)*

Although Paisley looms, including the Jacquards, were much more mechanical than Kashmir looms, they were not powerlooms. They required no other power than that of the workers themselves. The Paisley looms could be installed anywhere; they were not dependent upon sources of power. When Jacquards were used in factories, there was still no source of power other than the weaver. Yet controversy exists whether the shawls should be considered handwoven.

The fly-shuttle seems to be of crucial importance in making this determination. Shawl looms were unusually wide because the shawls were so wide. With such wide warps, a weaver was unable to throw the shuttle from one selvage to the other; the shuttle lodged somewhere in the middle. To propel it the rest of the distance, the weaver would have had to keep changing his position at the loom. Otherwise, two weavers, or a weaver and two children, were required to work side by side to get the shuttle across. To facilitate the process, a fly-shuttle, which could be conveniently operated by the weaver, was used in Paisley to propel the weft yarn from one side to the other.

This device, sometimes known as the "fly-shuttle attachment" was invented in 1733. It allows a spring to propel the shuttle across the loom when the weaver jerks a handle with his hand. It enables a weaver to produce twice as much in the same working time. Many weavers have resisted using the fly-shuttle because they consider the cloth no longer handwoven. Mary Atwater, when she was active in reviving handweaving in the United States during the first half of this century, rejected the fly-shuttle as a part of handweaving, even though she embraced mechanical looms. Many other weavers, however, feel that the fly-shuttle has nothing to do with whether a textile is handwoven or machinewoven: that the distinction lies elsewhere, that the fly-shuttle is no more than a convenient device for throwing a shuttle across a wide piece of weaving, and that the weaver has the same control over his work whether he throws the shuttle by hand or propels it across with a fly-shuttle. Paisley shawls were woven with the fly-shuttle.

5. The Designs

How the shawls became European expressions

The earliest fragment of a Cashmere shawl preserved in a public collection was woven in 1680. It shows a narrow border enclosing the entire textile and, at each end, framing a panel of simple plants. These are regularly spaced against an empty background. Despite the enclosing border, everything seems spacious and open. Small flowers in the narrow border are severely conventionalized, while the larger plants at the ends are semi-naturalistic. A conventionalized flower seems lifted from the border to become part of the semi-naturalistic plant. The mixture of the conventionalized and the somewhat

74

naturalistic, and the change in scale from one area to another are prominent features of the fragment.

The gentle plant, isolated against the empty background, speaks with unusual force. In its entirety—buds, stems, flowers, leaves, roots—it has special meaning, like Tennyson's flower in the crannied wall, "I hold you here, roots and all, in my hand." The viewer is aware of his own relationship to the plant and also the weaver's relationship to it. The plant grew within the narrow range of the weaver's stance at the loom; he could see it as an entity within a larger woven composition.

Surprisingly, this early Cashmere fragment recalls the charming bits of embroidery from Kashmir that today are sometimes regarded as deplorable tourist items. After the lavish displays of skillful handwork that characterize the late nineteenth century Cashmeres, today's scarfs appear minimal and meager. They have a naive openness and pale, pretty colors, often light pink and light blue against an undyed background. Yet the casual stitches are able to do what the early fragment does: describe simple isolated flowers that, by their presence, accent the wonderful woven fiber.

It is apparent from the fragment that the semi-naturalistic plant was not designed on the loom but was worked from a painted or printed design. The outlining suggests a painted line or a blockprint. It looks like a drawing filled in with color.

Twill-tapestry fragment of a Cashmere shawl from about 1680. The characteristic features of the plants are all clearly described as in illustrations in early European herbals—indeed, art historians are today tracing such motives in the art of the Near East and India to European sources. (Crown copyright: Victoria & Albert Museum)

(Above) Sketch of a brocaded silk sash, about 1700, probably from West India (Surat). A reproduction of this early textile can be found in Banaras Brocades, *by Krishna (page 13).*

(Right) Detail of brocaded silk from Benares, India, nineteenth century. The brocaded motive against a plain silk ground is typical of drawloom weaving using a comber repeat. Arranged in a half-drop and spaced close together, the motives create a background that is positive and active. The distribution of colors in horizontal bands is typical of brocade patterning.
    Paisley-type shawls could avoid such color distribution; colors could appear anywhere over the shawl. (Crown copyright: Victoria & Albert Museum)

What is most arresting about the fragment is that, although it is woven in twill-tapestry like the later Cashmere shawls, it looks like drawloom weaving. A silk brocaded sash, woven on a drawloom in Surat at about the same time that the Cashmere fragment was woven, shows similar narrow borders of flowers enclosing a border of spaced plant forms. The Cashmere fragment and the Surat sash are so alike it seems that one textile is imitating the other. It seems reasonable to assume that someone wanted the silk brocade patterns to be rendered in Cashmere fiber, since the colors of the Cashmere fragment are distributed as they logically would be in drawloom brocading, and since plant forms are repeated as they would be when threaded on what is called a "comber" repeat in a drawloom. (The comber repeat, named after the comber board, an essential part of a drawloom, keeps repeating motives identically, side by side.) Imitation of drawloom patterns, with their mechanical perfection, balance, and pleasing repetition, was not new in textile history; the splendid patterns had often been translated into other techniques such as embroidery and blockprinting.

Perhaps the Cashmere goat fiber was tried on the drawloom and didn't work. The drawloom was hard on warp yarns; it worked best with strong, smooth, elastic yarns such as silk. The Cashmere fiber was notoriously delicate, requiring the use of special tools even for simple weaving. The looms used in Kashmir for weaving the fiber had to be especially designed to minimize tension and friction. It has been suggested that, when Kashmir weavers turned to tapestry, they chose twill-tapestry because it was easier on the fiber than was plain weave tapestry.

If it is true that the early Cashmere shawls were imitating silk brocades (no one can say for certain, but anyone can speculate), then it would seem quite predictable that the plant form on the early fragment would look like a painted or printed design. For silk brocades were not designed directly on the loom as were so many other traditional textiles. Instead, they were worked from sketches and drawings. This was necessary because the drawloom required patterns to be threaded into the mechanism before the actual weaving commenced. Because they derive from drawn or painted designs and conform to certain limitations of the loom, drawloom patterns are unique and easily recognized.

In his work on Kashmir shawls, John Irwin, the English authority on the history of Indian textiles, refers to the Cashmeres as brocade-weaving. He says that "the technique of Kashmir shawl-brocading is known to the historians as the twill tapestry weave."[20] The statement is thoroughly confusing since brocade and tapestry are two separate and basic textile techniques. Yet the confusion serves to connect the Cashmere shawls to both the drawloom brocades and the twill tapestry.

Upon seeing the early Cashmere shawls, the Europeans must have immediately sensed the connection to drawloom patterns. Transposing them back to the drawloom probably seemed a very obvious solution to imitating the fashionable shawls.

The early Cashmere fragment indicates a narrow border surrounding the shawl, an end border, a narrow border above the end border, and a main rectangular field. These are standard in many textiles from India. Saris, sashes, scarfs and shawls are divided into such rectangles, some with a horizontal axis, some with a vertical axis. The shifts in axis direction animate an entire textile. The borders establish compartments for various patterns. The mechanical grid accents the horizontal-vertical nature of the woven structure and imparts a sense of calculated control.

Although early Paisley-type shawls retained these divisions, such compartments tended to disappear. With them went some of the formality and control that characterize the early shawls, especially those from Norwich. The clearcut divisions, which were such an essential feature of early Cashmeres and Paisley-types, tended to vanish in exuberant patterning that could not be restrained. Changes in women's costumes and ways of wearing the shawl—as

The back and front of a silk brocaded shawl, Kashmir, late nineteenth century. Most of the motives are brocaded with separate wefts, a very slow weaving process related to Kashmir tapestry weaving. Here, though, the patterns are determined mechanically on a drawloom, making them all identical and "mechanical." Because all the pattern wefts were inserted by hand, long floats and clipped ends were avoided. (Collection: Program in Visual Design, University of California, Berkeley)

Woven Paisley-type shawl with an unusual center indicating where the shawl was to be folded. The wearer had the choice of a plain black center or a multicolored patterned center around the neck. Paisley-type shawls departed from the conventional organization of borders and panels in order to: display the elaborate patterning to best advantage when the shawls were being worn; make the garments fit across the shoulders; keep the backs of the textiles from showing when they were folded and draped; and make them reveal different patterns on each side when folded. The results are often eccentric shapes and eccentric distributions of patterning, without the clear logic of the original bordered rectangles of cloth. (Collection: Marie Chesley)

the shawl became not only a fashionable garment but also a ceremonial textile—required new distribution of patterning. Patterns were placed where they would be most effective when folded and draped. Many late shawls, both Cashmere and Paisley-type, when laid out flat show not the orderly compartments of a ruled grid, but eccentric assemblages of front parts of weaving alongside back parts of weaving, patched together so that fronts and backs appear on the same surface and neither side can be surely designated as the front or the back. The clarity and certainty of the early Cashmere organization give way to this sort of makeshift expedience. When the garments were worn, the patterns fell into place according to plan. Now, when they are laid out flat, they suggest not beautiful textile rectangles from the loom but the cut and assembled garments of Europe.

Such combinations of front and back pieces were resorted to because neither Cashmere nor Paisleys were reversible in the sense that the weaving was good on both sides. Since they were often worn folded, the front and back of the shawls showed simultaneously. While this difficulty was somewhat overcome by assembling fronts and backs, weavers kept working on reversible shawls. Toward the end of the Paisley industry, such shawls were perfected, but they appeared too late.

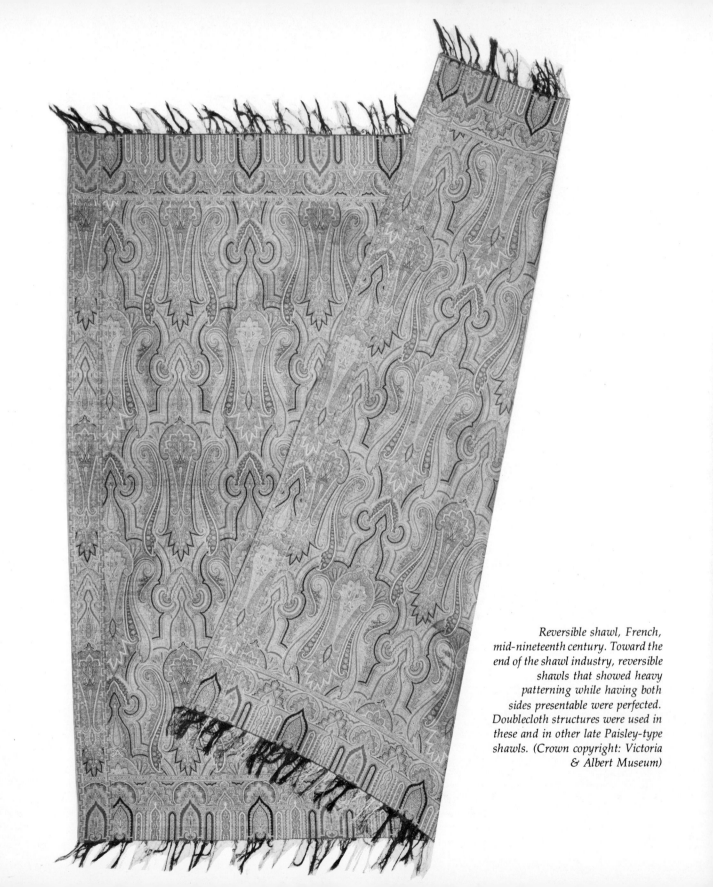

Reversible shawl, French, mid-nineteenth century. Toward the end of the shawl industry, reversible shawls that showed heavy patterning while having both sides presentable were perfected. Doublecloth structures were used in these and in other late Paisley-type shawls. (Crown copyright: Victoria & Albert Museum)

Whereas earlier shawls emphasized the end panels, which hung below the wearer's waist, later shawls emphasized the great central panel. Often a medallion appeared in the very center of the shawl; sometimes this medallion was filled with intricate patterns, and sometimes it was left plain, surrounded and defined by pattern. In both cases this medallion, when folded, formed a sort of collar around the wearer's neck, like the cloud collars of Chinese garments.

The simple, straightforward plant motive that decorates the early Cashmere fragment gradually becomes less naturalistic, more formalized in both the Cashmere and the Paisley-type shawls. It assumes a simpler, smoother contour filled with floral details. All the features of leaves, flowers, stems, buds, remain easily identifiable. Each motive, now called a Paisley, is quite symmetrical along the central axis of the plant's stem, with a slight tipping at the very top. This tipping has a life quality, like an unfolding leaf that is straightening, becoming rigid. The plant seems to be striving to achieve perfect symmetry.

Paisley-type shawl with applied printed bands. This shawl of green handspun wool was designed to be worn folded, with the curved corner overlaying the squared corner. The border is carefully pieced, with patches outlined in red and white couching. (Shawl belonged to Frances Ellen Steward. Collection: Pioneer Museum, Salt Lake City)

(Below) Detail of Flemish tapestry, La Mise au Tombeau, *sixteenth century. The tapestry technique is used to represent a silk pattern that includes the motives, the scallops and serrated foliage; these were to appear densely overlapped and embellished in the Paisley-type shawls. Patterns that were stated clearly and directly in sixteenth century textiles appeared in Paisleys 200 years later in involved and intricate transformations. (Collection: Cluny Museum, Paris)*

(Above, left) Detail of a child's dress, Turkish, sixteenth century. Motives resembling those that became known as Paisleys were used for centuries in the textiles of the Near East and India. In this silk pattern, stylized flowers appear as they were to appear later in Paisley-type shawls. Ribbon-like petals of large flowers are filled with a multitude of small flowers. Elongated flowers, like heads of wheat, show the serrated contours that were to become familiar in Paisley shawls. Curving branches of flowers, each with six perfect petals, appeared in European velvets, brocades, and tapestries, and later, in Paisleys. (Crown copyright: Victoria & Albert Museum)

The motive is not unique to Cashmere shawls but appears conspicuously in decorative arts of Persia, India, Turkey, and Central Asia. Sometimes it is without any floral content. Other times it is one large flower or a cluster of flowers all compactly arranged. The flowers are the well-loved carnation, rose, tulip, plum, lotus, and palm.

How strange that in the West this motive is known so generally by the name of a town in Scotland! Yet the motive's source is sometimes traced to European herbals, books describing plants, sent to be copied in India or the Middle East. The Paisley has been variously described as a cone, mango, pine, teardrop, leaf, cypress, sperm, pear. Frequently people ask for an explanation of the shape. They want a meaning apart from the decorative. Is it a fertility symbol, a tree of life? Art historians are trying to find answers, to trace the motive's development and significance. With certainty it can be said that the motive expresses a life quality. And that today it is unique in providing the joy of recognition of an ancient decorative motive to countless people who are quite unfamiliar with other such design motives.

Motives from various textiles of the Near East and India indicating the transition from isolated flower forms to the compact pine or Paisley form and the changes inspired by the twill-tapestry technique. These were sketched from textiles in the collections of the Victoria & Albert Museum and the Program in Visual Design and Robert H. Lowie Museum of Anthropology, University of California, Berkeley.

In some of the early end panels, secondary shapes decorate the background spaces between the plants. These shapes are called "fill ornaments" or "fills." In time they expand until only a narrow line of background remains between them and the main motive. Motives and fills are manipulated and distorted to fit together compactly yet not touch or overlap. All the shapes accommodate each other. Everything fits like a puzzle. Instead of floral patterns appearing on a plain background, flowing lines of background seem to appear against a dense floral texture. Movement occurs through the background spaces rather than within the motives with their elaborate embellishments. The figures and ground have exchanged roles.

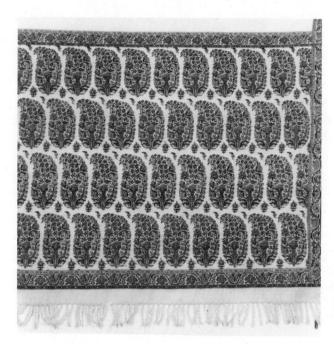

(Left) Although this Paisley-type woven plaid of monumental proportions (about 5' x 10') appears to have borders added, it was actually woven in one piece. The large area of cones shows the rows staggered to create diagonal movement. Each cone is quite symmetrical except for the tip, which is a branch of leaves and flowers bent to the left. Fill ornaments reduce the background space to create a lively white line of rather uniform width moving through the weaving. (Collection: Robert H. Lowie Museum of Anthropology, University of California, Berkeley)

(Right) The cones in this Paisley-type shawl are arranged like those in the above figure, but a more static effect is created because the background has been filled in almost completely with a decorative texture of flowers, leaves and branches, which allows only a narrow white line to surround each cone. The movement is not flowing. Errors in the weaving show prominently where one band of cones ends and the next begins, and even more at the top of the illustration where a number of treadlings have been skipped altogether, suggesting that a drawboy lost his place in drawing the cords. The weaver could not detect such errors until the weaving was complete since he saw only the back of the shawl as he wove. Needless to say the boys were severely reprimanded for errors which reduced the value of the shawls. (Collection: Robert H. Lowie Museum of Anthropology, University of California, Berkeley)

This early Paisley-type shawl, with a custom stamp of 1823, shows a large end border with comber repeats skillfully manipulated in the weaving to vary the color in the repeated motives. (Courtesy: Honolulu Academy of Arts, Gift of Mrs. Robert Morton and Mrs. J. A. Veech)

Sometimes the compartments at the ends of the shawls are filled with several rows of repeated cones or plant motives. The cones are made to fit together in a half-drop arrangement leaving diagonals between to create a lively sort of trellis. The cones of one row tip right, the cones of the next row tip left. Somehow the cones or plants, which once stood separately with such authority, are reduced to background. Later they are negated in other ways. Large cones, densely elaborated, overlap each other and become entwined and then fragmented. The familiar motives appear as no more than snatches of curves submerged in dots of color that are in truth tiny flowers and branches all contrived of shapes fitting together like miniature mosaics.

In early shawls the large central rectangle is often a plain, undecorated area of elegant twill. Sometimes this rectangle is enhanced by small floral motives, often quite abstract, regularly spaced in an all over pattern. Very early Paisleys use this all over distribution of small motives. These were called "spade center shawls" because the spots resembled the pips on playing cards. Since these small motives are often sprigs of leaves and flowers, the patterned areas were referred to as "sprigged," just as similar areas were referred to in European silk brocades.

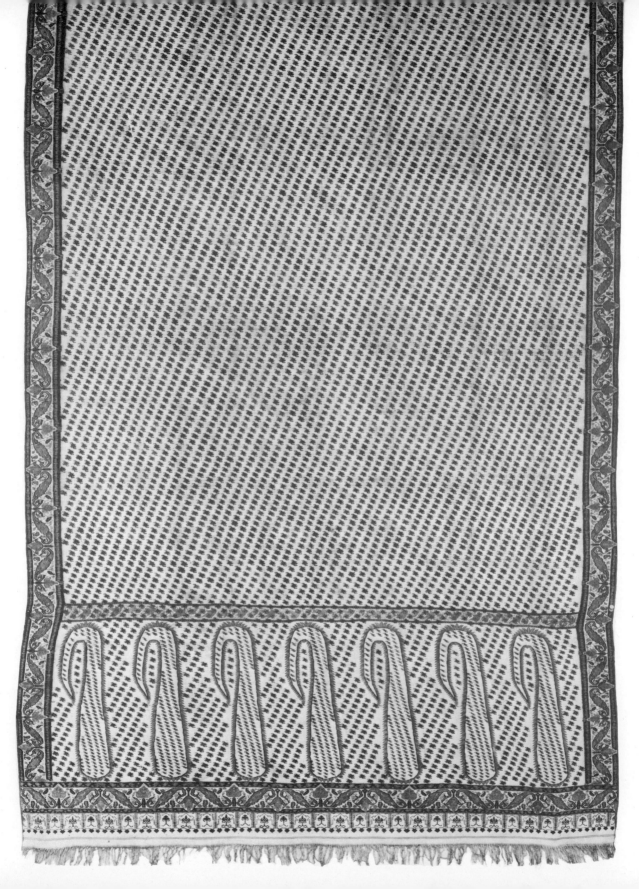

Sometimes the large rectangle shows a complex all over pattern, like a piece of printed yardage, to which borders were attached; the patterns are not adjusted to fit the rectangle but give the sensation of running off on all sides and of being quite accidentally chopped off by the borders. Sometimes the large rectangle is empty except for small motives tucked in each corner. These corner motives, which were expensive to weave, became larger, more flowing, extending toward the center of the shawl.

(Opposite) Cashmere twill-tapestry shawl, eighteenth–nineteenth century. Here the pine motive is not the flowing curves achieved in printing and in weaving with many fine threads, but is angular and distorted, as the motive often appeared in ikat dyeing and pile techniques. Paisley-type shawls with spotted fields like this were called "spade center" because the small patterns suggested spots on playing cards. In this Cashmere, the large cone motives are quite unrelated to the flowing outer border design. Between the border and the fringe is a delicate band of motives like the embroidered tabs that were prominent features of embroidered patchwork Cashmeres and that inspired Paisley weavers to remarkable technical accomplishments. (Crown copyright: Victoria & Albert Museum)

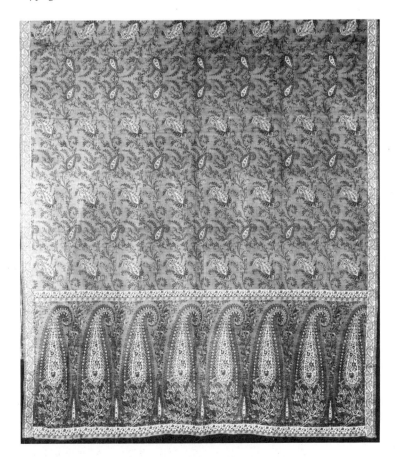

British woven shawl, 1830. Early Paisley-type shawls woven on the harness loom with the help of a drawboy were limited in their patterning—a pattern could be intricate but could not spread over an entire shawl as required in the 1850s. Often the early shawls were woven as separate components to be sewed together by women workers. In this way the desired variety and quantity of pattern was achieved. Motives could fill a wide space only by repeating. Consequently, the end panels show motives repeated identically six or eight times, as in this example. In the early shawls the large center field was often left plain. When patterned, it sometimes carried a small repeated motive, as in the spade center shawls, and sometimes it showed an allover repeat pattern, as in this example. (Crown copyright: Victoria & Albert Museum)

Some shawls woven in twill-tapestry are boldly striped, very Turkish in appearance in contrast to the delicate florals that look so thoroughly Persian. When such stripes were copied in Paisley, they were called zebras (pronounced zebb-ras). The stripes are often overlaid with intertwining patterns, a sort of strapwork, moving from one stripe to the next in a dense mechanical structure. Embellished stripes are further elaborated with large medallions and sections of medallions overlaying the stripes, suggesting a transparency of the greatest complexity. The zebra shawls with medallions recall the Mexican saltillo serapes.

(Left) Near Eastern shawl, described as a Cashmere, woven in the twill-tapestry technique, nineteenth century. Scroll-like motives are superimposed over the stripes, with secondary motives adjusting to both the stripes and the scrolls. (Collection: Program in Visual Design, University of California, Berkeley)

(Right) Printed Paisley shawl. This large wool shawl—about six feet wide—shows narrow printed stripes of yellow, blue, red, brown, and white, imitating the Turkish models and emphasizing the twill. Striped Paisley shawls were known as "zebras." Many were imitations of Turkish shawls. Gradually, these Paisleys were embellished heavily with the same motives that appear in the borders of other Paisley shawls. (Collection: Paisley Museum and Art Galleries)

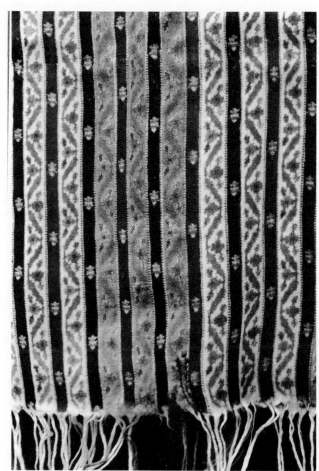

The color of the early Cashmere fragment is simple and restrained. Since tapestry as a technique imposes no restrictions on the number of colors or where they can appear, later Cashmere shawls showed more colors to satisfy Europeans. Each area of color appears as a shape with clearly defined contours. Shapes do not merge together; they are not shaded as in European tapestry; and they are not blended to create colors. The individual mosaic-like shapes are angular, jagged, and tipped because of the distortions imposed by the twill-tapestry technique. The technique gives a slight raised edge to each shape where colors join. When these color effects were attempted in Paisley-type shawls, the results were quite different. The mosaic shapes were copied, but without the surrounding ridge; the Paisley shapes became extremely flat. While a patch of red in a Cashmere pattern was created by a red yarn moving back and forth in a specified area, a patch of red in a Paisley was created by wefts that moved all the way from one selvage to the other. The same red weft could be made to appear in many places across the width of the warp. This encouraged the use of many small shapes. Color areas became broken into thousands upon thousands of tiny flowers, twigs and stems—which the wearer of the shawl perhaps identified at close range but which, from even a short distance, blended into a variegated texture. Unlike the Cashmeres, which could show any number of colors in their patterns, the Paisleys could show only a limited number. By using these in small bits, the designers were able to create color effects of great variety and beauty. Even though the late Paisley shawls appear hard, flat, mechanical and impersonal, they seem at the same time evasive and impressionistic with their tiny flickering bits of color.

Printed zebra-type Paisley shawl, showing the same border patterns that appear in other Paisley shawls. (Collection: Paisley Museum and Art Galleries)

French shawl, printed silk, nineteenth century. This shawl is divided into compartments, one showing the zebra pattern set on the diagonal, the other showing an allover pattern with medallions. The corner has been curved and carefully fringed. (The Metropolitan Museum of Art, Gift of Mrs. C. Klingenstein and Mrs. M. J. Breitenbach, 1938)

(Opposite) Twill-tapestry Cashmere-type shawl. The striped textile includes end borders that allow the stripes to show through the pattern. A center medallion shows the stripes moving through its dense pattern. (Collection: Program in Visual Design, University of California, Berkeley)

Woven Paisley-type shawl, Scottish, early 1820s. The sprig-like motives are used to embellish the background around the border motives. When Paisley shawls became even more complex in their patterning, this distribution of motives was superimposed onto zebra stripes. (Crown copyright: Victoria & Albert Museum)

(Below) Woven shawl, Scottish, 1820s–1830s. Here sections of the central medallion are fit into the corners. The patterns in the stripes are a mixture of motives. The medallions appear transparent, superimposed on the striped background. The result is dense, heavy patterning. (Crown copyright: Victoria & Albert Museum)

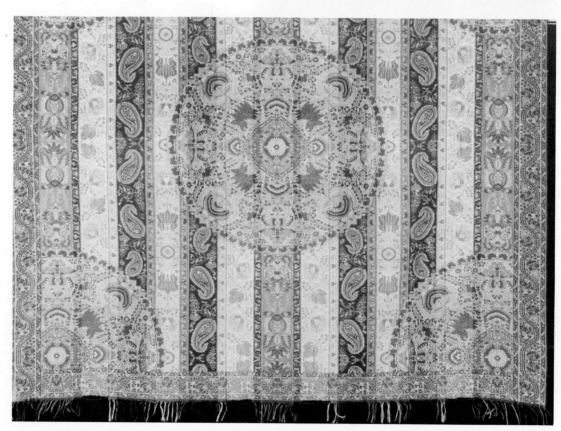

Saltillo Sarape, nineteenth century Mexican. Like so many of the early Paisley shawls, the ground has a dense covering of small, regularly spaced motives, enclosed by borders. A complex medallion seems to be applied onto the patterned ground. Scottish weavers were undoubtedly familiar with Mexican sarapes; when the shawl industry died, Paisley weavers wove ponchos for the Latin American market late in the nineteenth century. (The Metropolitan Museum of Art, Gift of Mrs. Russell Sage, 1910)

(Right) Kashan (Persian) rug. The same patterning appears in the Cashmere patchwork shawls and also in the Paisley-type shawls. When Jacquards made it possible to weave large, complex and flowing patterns, inspiration for the new shawls came from rugs of the Near East and India, embroidered patchwork Cashmeres, and traditional European rug patterns of embellished intertwining curves. (Reproduced from Decorative Textiles, *by George Leland Hunter)*

(Left) Patchwork Cashmere shawl showing the same distribution of motives as the Kashan rug. (Collection: Robert H. Lowie Museum of Anthropology, University of California, Berkeley)

When patterns that were designed for European looms were woven as twill-tapestry in India, tapestry was obliged to produce tiny spots and dashes of color rather than the clearly articulated shapes so natural to the technique. The backs of the shawls became dense, tangled networks of many yarns moving from spot to spot as required by the designs. The reverse sides of all the shawls—the twill-tapestry Cashmeres, the embroidered patchwork Cashmeres, and the Paisley-type shawls—show energetic yarns in dense, uncontrived configurations. The floating or clipped yarns layer the back surfaces, almost concealing the weaving. Colors intermix in glorious textural effects. Yarns are revealed as individual spun elements. The effects are truly fibrous.

(Left) Detail of a Cashmere patchwork shawl with embroidered tabs patched onto a twill-tapestry section that is astonishingly similar in appearance to Paisley weaving. The embroidery appears bold in scale and somewhat crude in relation to the extremely refined weaving. In the upper section of the illustration, the tapestry is patched from woven pieces of irregular shapes. This patching was used to achieve dramatic contrasts in value that the Paisley-type shawls were never quite able to match. (Collection: Program in Visual Design, University of California, Berkeley)

(Above) Detail of Paisley woven shawl. The tabs around the edges became a prominent feature of Paisley-type shawls. Tabs occurred quite naturally in Cashmere patchwork shawls, with many pieces of cloth assembled into a single textile. The effect was imitated in Paisley-type shawls through dyeing, printing and weaving. In this photograph, special dyeing of the warps is evident where the white fades out above the white rectangle. This dyeing was apparently done in two ways: either the warp was stretched on a frame and dyed before it was put on the loom or it was stained on the loom. The arched motive inside the rectangles recalls the embroidered motives in the Cashmere tabs, although the freedom of the embroidery has been replaced by a mechanical rigidity. (Collection: Paisley Museum and Art Galleries)

(Right) Silk samples found in a pattern book from Spitalfields, England, 1784. This special dyeing technique, which was used in the fancy silks of Lyon and Spitalfields, was also used in Paisley. It relates to the special dyeing of the warps in the shawl industry. In these samples, the dyeing was a prominent feature that was accentuated by the weaving, whereas in the Paisley shawls the dyeing was altogether inconspicuous. (Crown copyright: Victoria & Albert Museum)

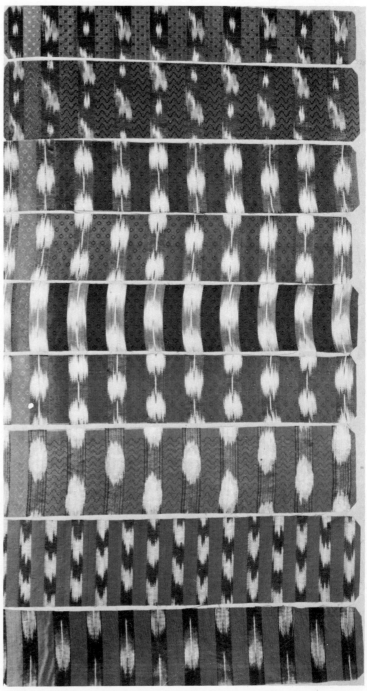

(Above, left) Detail of printed Paisley shawl. The dense patterning appears on silk gauze with satin stripes; the striping is conspicuous in all the unprinted areas, animating them. While the motives were derived from woven shawls, the silk gauze shawls were not imitations and did not represent themselves as woven patterns. The border recalls the Cashmere shawls with embroidery extending partly down the patchwork tabs. (Collection: Paisley Museum and Art Galleries)

To imitate the appearance of the tabs and fringes of Cashmere patchwork shawls, the warps for Paisley-type shawls were specially dyed in relation to the patterns that would be woven on them. In the areas where the finished shawls would show white tabs, the Paisley warps had to be white. Where pale blue tabs would be woven, the warps had to be pale blue. But then, further along in the weaving, these same white and pale blue warp threads had to be black or red. The various colors were dyed into the warps, not in stripes but in patches of color precisely relating to the pattern of the finished shawl. An unwoven warp on a loom showed roughly the color areas that the weft patterns would define. A weaver had to be able to control his beat to fit the required number of wefts into the allotted dyed space. He could not add extra wefts, or eliminate any, since the number of wefts was established in the draws. Hand-weavers were required to maintain the absolute regularity of beat that characterized the new powerweaving. In very good shawls, the special dyeing can scarcely be detected, so perfectly does the weaving fit the dyeing. In less successful shawls, the dyed color can be seen flowing through the patterns into areas where it doesn't belong. The dyeing was the work of specialists. Unfortunately this remarkable aspect of the Paisley industry has not been well documented. Such dyeing of a warp and then matching a patterning weft to it is most unusual in European weaving—indeed in weaving worldwide. It relates to ikated and warp-printed silks which were popular in Europe; in these textiles, however, the dyeing is a dominant feature in the finished work whereas in Paisleys the dyeing is almost indiscernible, merely supporting other patterning.

For many years the patterns in European textiles for court and church, and for wealthy upper classes, were curvilinear, against the grain of direct horizontal-vertical patterning. As it became possible for the middle and lower classes to have more textiles, they wanted curved patterns, not only because of fashion's interest in the sinuous and flowing, but also because of the identification of such patterns with upper classes. It is not surprising that Paisley shawls for the new mass market became extravagant indulgences in intertwining curves.

Arbitrary changes in patterns were made to keep the garments fashionable—always new and different, yet always recognizably the same. Design sources were astonishingly varied. The cone motive, which appeared with such authority in the early shawls, often became an incidental feature. By the time Paisley shawls had reached the midpoint in their history, their design influence came mainly from France rather than from India. The shawls were truly European expressions. Motives from earlier silk designs of Europe became prominent in the shawls—especially the lace motives and the branches of

98

flowers that were so popular and pretty. Drafted details, often heavy, static and formal, which characterized the contemporary design of furniture, books, household utensils and architectural ornaments, became dominant in scroll motives and shawl borders, appearing alongside the feathery naturalistic flowers. A single shawl incorporated any number of design impulses and historical references. Today the results are often regarded as a deplorable mishmash of imagery. Motives from the great textiles of the world were transformed into the mechanical and the complex. Yet the audacity of the combinations, and the resulting transformations, provide many visual delights and surprises—certain shawls seem at the same time stately and eternal, and outrageously capricious.

(Opposite) Flemish tapestry, second half of sixteenth century, woven in wool and silk. This shows the European preoccupation with curves and subtle shadings derived from drawings and paintings. The effects challenged the technical skills of the weavers. The entanglement of forms, the extensions of foliage from the borders into the central panel, the elimination of the background, the delicate floral sprays set amidst large serrated leaves all characterize the late Paisley-type shawls. (The Metropolitan Museum of Art, Rogers Fund, 1906)

Savonnerie rug, seventeenth century Europe. The intertwining scrolls interspersed with flowers were long familiar in European decorative art. As Paisley-type shawls departed more and more from the early Cashmere designs, French designers attempted to satisfy European taste, injecting motives and details, and organizations of motives, which were already popular in European decorative art: lace effects, bands or straps of lace undulating, interweaving through other motives; bands embellished with floral motives, crossing over established boundaries of borders and central fields. The complexity and detail increased. (Reproduced from Decorative Textiles *by George Leland Hunter)*

Mechanical improvements encouraged new designs; new designs stimulated mechanical improvements. The quest for larger patterns brought reluctant acceptance of the Jacquard in Paisley. This device offered unknown opportunities, not only for large compositions and flowing curves, but for juxtapositions of woven structures appropriate to the juxtapositions of imagery. Structurally, many of the late Paisleys departed from the earlier shawls. Like so many of today's commercial or industrial textiles, which the Paisleys undoubtedly influenced, the late shawls were often complex combinations of weaves: doublecloths, twills, plain weaves. Always the weaving appeared diagrammatically controlled. Improvements in the looms' lay boxes permitted more colors and brought astonishing color effects. The early Paisley loom with its fly-shuttle could handle three or four pattern shuttles, meaning that only three or four different colors could appear in the pattern. Later looms were able to handle eight to ten shuttles. The wondrous mechanisms were constantly being made responsive to the spirit of the times that fostered an abundant display of decoration.

(Left) Carpet woven in Durham, England, 1851. This carpet, which was exhibited at the Crystal Palace Exhibition in London, shows the same drafted curves, appearing amidst leafy branches, that were to characterize the late Paisley-type shawls. (From The Crystal Palace Exhibition, Illustrated Catalogue, London, 1851)

(Right) Printed Paisley shawl. Flowing through the overlapping pine motives are embellished bands or straps that destroy the isolation of the separate motives. The tiny mosaic-like shapes are used to create a lacy effect. The lace, scallops, and ribbons, with which the shawls had been worn since early in the century, appeared in the shawl patterns. (Collection: Paisley Museum and Art Galleries)

Hand-knotted carpet, Bullerswood, *by William Morris, 1889. After the Paisley shawl industry had ended, William Morris was intrigued with the same motives and the same organization of interweaving scrolls. (Crown copyright: Victoria & Albert Museum)*

Shawls kept reflecting not only the technological improvements but also the fashion changes and historical events. Longer shawls, which the crinolines required, brought larger patterns of flowing extended curves. Events influenced designs: the death of Charlotte, queen consort of George III of England, in 1818 popularized black center shawls for years, while the visit of George IV to Edinburgh in 1822 was responsible for a long continuing vogue for shawls called "Pale End," creamy white centers and borders of large blue pine motives.

Despite their responsiveness to changing times, Paisley shawls are impossible to date with any certainty. Available information would seem to be quite adequate: newspaper advertisements, government documents, the catalog of the Crystal Palace Exhibition, custom stamps on shawls, fashion illustrations, pattern books and dated designs, etc. Yet shawls woven in Paisley cannot be distinguished from those woven elsewhere in Britain, or from those woven in France. While it has been said that the town of Paisley was so successful in driving out competition that shawls can quite confidently be designated as Paisleys, the fact that such confidence is misplaced is abundantly clear when shawls known to be from various places are compared. While the tendency is to call all the European shawls "Paisleys," a very high percentage were certainly woven in France, which was such a leader in shawl manufacture and design.

Even the changing dimensions of the shawls do not offer reliable clues. Before Jacquards were woven in Paisley, some shawls were enormous. In about 1838 "red silk" shawls were ten feet long and twelve feet wide. These elegant garments of silk and Cashmere fiber could be so large because they were plain centered, with decorative borders woven separately and added. A shawl was woven in sixteen separate pieces.

During the late years the Jacquard shawls were primarily three sizes: those called "shawls" or "squares" were five feet square; those called "plaids" were ten feet or twelve feet long (the name does not mean that the pattern was a plaid, but rather that the shawls were long rectangles); those called "three-quarter plaids" were eight feet four inches long. Widths were five feet, which was the width of the looms. Differences in dimensions affected the patterns—the squares tended to have four similar formal borders from which motives moved freely inward, defining an open shape in the center. Plaids and three-quarter plaids had two similar ends, elaborately patterned, with extended forms reaching toward an open center. These ends usually emphasized the long axis of the shawl. Along with these large plaids and squares, smaller scarfs and stoles with the Paisley imagery were manufactured.

This is a gouache painting on paper copied from a shawl that was woven in Kashmir. Early in the nineteenth century, an Englishman, William Moorcraft, traveled in India where he commissioned a native painter to copy the cone motives from a number of existing shawls to inspire manufacturers in England. Eight of these wonderfully detailed renderings are known and are in the collection of the Metropolitan Museum of Art. This example was copied from a shawl woven for the Persian market. (The Metropolitan Museum of Art, The Elisha Whittelsey Fund, 1962)

Because of the methods of manufacture, with so many variations in equipment—old looms and new looms weaving old designs and new designs—dating remains uncertain. Since shawls acquired traditional meaning in society, certain designs became appropriate for certain occasions—baptisms, marriages, and so forth—the old flourished along with the new.

Early in the fashion, French artists were commissioned to design shawls based on the Cashmeres but without what were considered to be their confusion and bizarreness. Such French designs were woven in France and India, and also in Britain where they became models to be copied and pirated. Fortunately, many drawn and painted designs have been preserved in the Paisley Museum, which was founded in 1870, at the time when the industry was dying and records and materials from factories were being disposed of. The designs show individual motives and sections of shawls worked out on point paper, and color sketches on semi-transparent paper that is now extremely brittle and fragile. The background color was painted on the back side of the paper, while the patterns were painted on the front. The background color showing through everywhere in a subdued way creates a full rich color effect. Specialists painted these to give an idea of the appearance of the shawls and to instruct those working out the color notations.

Painted design for striped Paisley shawl. For various purposes, patterns were copied from cloth. Since tracing paper was not available, transparent paper was made by brushing sweet oil over tissue paper until it was thoroughly wet. When the paper dried, the tracing could be made with pencil. Sometimes the drawing was then transferred to clean drawing paper and colored. This design is painted on oiled paper, with the background color painted on the back of the paper. By now, the paper is brittle, while the paint is flaking from the oily surface. This was submitted for copyright in 1843. (Collection: Paisley Museum and Art Galleries)

(Above) Pattern books preserved in the Paisley Museum show painted designs and sketches of isolated motives and repeats. The large drafts for weaving the shawls from such patterns were not preserved. (Collection: Paisley Museum and Art Galleries)

(Left) Blockprinted Paisley design copyrighted in 1848. To discourage the pirating of designs, a system was developed for registering designs with the Designs Office in London. Copyright was granted for nine months. A print of the blocks on cloth is shown here affixed to the certificate. (Collection: Paisley Museum and Art Galleries)

In the early days of the shawl industry some Paisley weavers were able to do their own designing. A few years later this was no longer true. Artists who were not weavers made designs that weavers then rendered into fiber. The work became increasingly specialized.

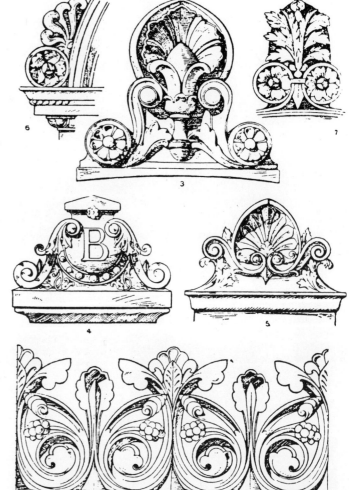

(This page) The patterning of Paisley shawls is usually approached through investigation of Cashmere shawls and other Near Eastern Textiles. It could as profitably be approached through study of nineteenth century British ornamental work and architecture. Design students in nineteenth century Britain were taught to adapt and combine Greek, Roman, Egyptian, Elizabethan, Gothic, French, etc., ornament. Such mixtures appear in Paisley shawls. A surprising number of motives were taken from Greek ornament, which was popular in all the decorative arts. The acanthus became conspicuous, elongated, interlocked, modified to fit spaces. (From A Handbook of Ornament by Franz Sales Meyer)

(Opposite, bottom left) Woven silk shawl, English, about 1815–20. At the same time that woolen shawls were imitating those from Kashmir, silk shawls were continuing the European tradition of naturalistic florals that had reached such perfection and refinement in French and English brocades. These motives gradually became incorporated into the Paisley-type shawls. (Crown copyright: Victoria & Albert Museum)

(Top right) Printed Paisley-type shawl brought from England in 1855 by Mary Coucune Wasden. Chinese motives are combined with traditional Paisley borders. To satisfy the demand for Cashmeres, textiles from Turkey, Persia, and China were imported and often sold as Cashmeres. These goods were available to be copied, consumed, enjoyed, wondered at. Everything could be used without reservation, understanding, or modest restraint. The world's art was a sort of smorgasbord. Something could be taken from here, something from there, all to be set together—the Gothic, Celtic, Moresque, Chinese, Indian, Turkish, Persian. (Collection: Pioneer Museum, Salt Lake City)

(Right) Printed wool fabric designed by a company artist and manufactured in Mulhouse between 1830 and 1840. The pine motive embellished with floral extensions is alternated with naturalistic flower garlands and imitations of ikated silk ribbon or silk chiné. In a remarkable way the so-different patterns seem to penetrate each other. The result is exuberant and overflowing. (From Persian Textiles, Second Series by Hans Carl Perleberg)

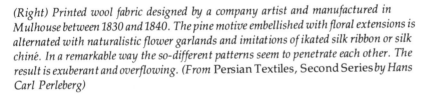

English shawl, about 1850. At the same time that
Paisley-type shawls were fashionable, other quite
different shawls were also popular. This rather coarse
wool twill is blockprinted in various colors with the
bouquets that characterized so much decorative art of the
period. Designers were advised to spend their leisure time
gathering flowers and grouping them in various
combinations. They were also advised to cultivate flower
gardens. (Collection: Paisley Museum and Art Galleries)

Detail of Paisley printed shawl, from about 1840, a time
when naturalistic flowers appeared prominently in both
woven and printed patterns. (Collection: Paisley
Museum and Art Galleries)

Printed shawl from Mulhouse, 1810. The trailing
semi-naturalistic flowers, with each petal showing a
highlight and shadow to impart a three-dimensionality,
are combined with various decorative elements including
the pine motive, set in one corner of the central field. The
effect throughout is lacelike. Of special interest is the
manner in which the blocks have been fit together at the
corner of the wide border. (Courtesy: Musée de
l'Impression sur Etoffes de Mulhouse)

(Opposite, bottom) Shawl of pillow lace, Flemish, first half of nineteenth
century. Machine-made net is combined with handmade bobbin lace.
Floral bouquets of large flowers are surrounded by delicate branches and
tendrils reaching into the background, like the encirclements of the pine
motives in Paisley-type shawls. Decorative straps move through the
foliage, while drafted curves extend from one area to the next. (Crown
copyright: Victoria & Albert Museum)

(Above) Paisley-type woven shawl that incorporates the Greek scroll motive as a prominent feature. The wide tabs seem to have lost all connections with the tabs of Cashmere patchwork. (Collection: Robert H. Lowie Museum of Anthropology, University of California, Berkeley)

(Above) Detail of panel of brocaded silk, French, early eighteenth century. Patterns from French silks appeared a century later in Paisley-type shawls: the undulating ribbon-like bands filled with smaller motives of foliage; plant forms extending beyond their confines; lacy scallops outlining the curving bands; delicate foliage reaching into the background surrounding massive flowers. (Crown copyright: Victoria & Albert Museum)

(Right) Preliminary sketch or design for a woven Paisley shawl. The interlacing bands and the delicate transparent-appearing scallops are influenced by lace designs and silk brocades. The mixtures of styles and imagery in the late shawls are astonishing. (From The Paisley Shawl *by Matthew Blair)*

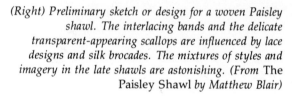

In India the twill-tapestry shawls were worked from painted designs. It was not a matter of following a cartoon the size of the finished shawl, in the way that European tapestry weavers follow a cartoon by placing a full-size drawing or photograph behind the warps, or draw the cartoon onto the warp threads. Instead the painted patterns were carefully transcribed by specialists into symbols that were written down on cards called talims. Weavers sat side by side at the loom, each with his area of warp to weave, while someone else read the instructions regarding intervals and colors. Reading from the talim was done in a singsong manner. The weavers watched the patterns emerge as they followed the instructions. Variations of this method are still used in Kashmir for weaving pile carpets. Patterns are said to be memorized like notations in music. Recited designs are passed from one generation to another. As far as the shawls were concerned, the method must have worked better for the small repeated patterns of the early textiles than for the elaborate late patterns.

(Opposite) Seven lithographs that were prepared to illustrate the system of codes for patterns and colors used by the shawl weavers in Kashmir. (Crown copyright: Victoria & Albert Museum)

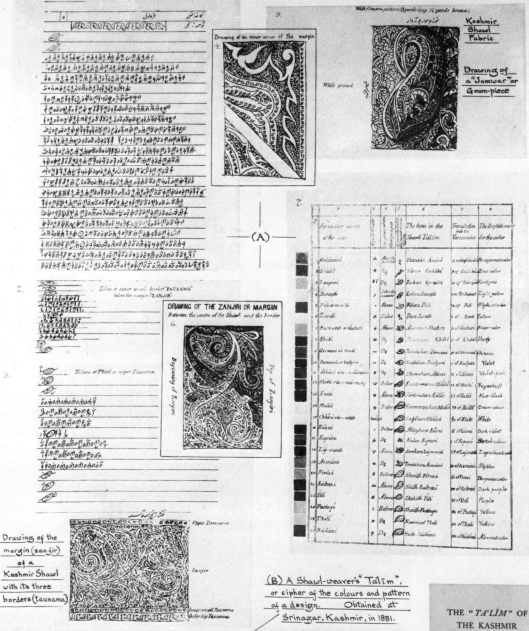

The "*TA'LÍM*" OF THE KASHMIR SHAWL-WEAVERS.

(A) Seven lithographs, plain and tinted, illustrating the *ta'lím* or code of the pattern and colour-scheme of a shawl.

(B) A *ta'lím* arranged by the designer's assistant (*tarah-band : tarahgurú*) from a black-and-white design. This written cipher was obtained at Srinagar, Kashmir, in 1881.

Given by C. Stanley Clarke, Esq.

I.M. 33–1924.

In Paisley, drawn or painted patterns were transferred by specialists onto graph paper: calculating each intersection of warp and weft, indicating colors and providing instructions to weavers. The weavers tied the patterns into the lashes that the drawboys later pulled to make the openings for the wefts. Since each weft row consisted of a number of colors, each color requiring a separate opening and a separate shuttle, the colors were figured and tied in the same order in which the shuttles were arranged in the lay boxes. The pattern was thus established in the loom, and from then on the instructions were no longer needed. By pulling the lashes in turn, and throwing the shuttles in order, the pattern was created.

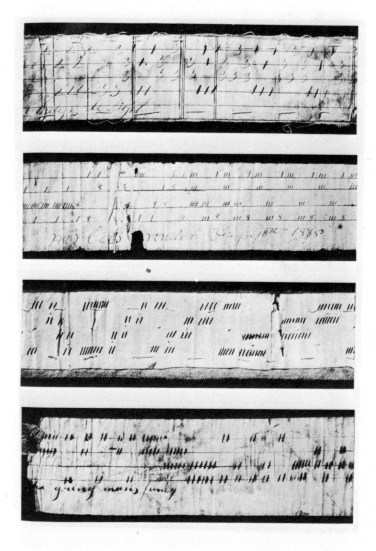

Old weaving drafts used in the Kentucky Mountains. The patterns for coverlets were transcribed into signs that instructed weavers about threading or programming the looms. Patterns could be recorded and remembered in this condensed form; they could also be transmitted from one weaver to another and from one generation to another. (From Book of Handwoven Coverlets *by Eliza Obenshain)*

Forty-five-inch section of weaving draft for a Paisley shawl labeled "Gasport shawl draft." Each square represents a crossing of a warp thread and a weft thread. Since each thread in the weaving had to be accounted for, drafts became enormous as shawls increased in size and complexity. A complete draft might have covered the floor of a large room. No complete drafts have been preserved in the Paisley Museum. (Collection: Paisley Museum and Art Galleries)

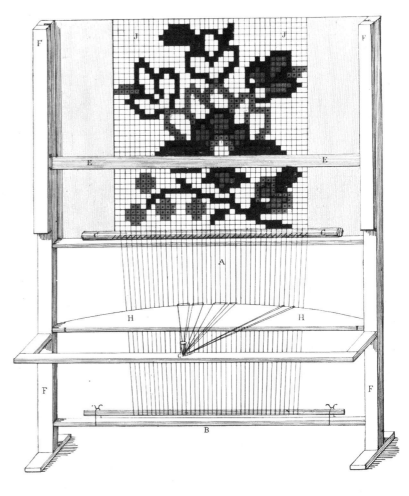

A simplified sketch showing how the design is programmed into the drawloom. The process, which required either two or three workers, was called "reading on the design," or "flower lashing." One man read the flower (the design), a second "took it down," and a third lashed it on. Here the design is squared off and mounted onto a frame called a lasher's frame. Extending below the design are cords corresponding to the separate warp threads on the loom. A ruler (E-E) is shown across the design; this marks the horizontal row directly under the ruler that is being lashed. Each color in each horizontal row requires a separate lash. The lash is tied to a peg at G. When the lash is pulled forward, all the cords tied to it move forward. When the lash is complete, it is slipped down out of the way. All the separate lashes that compose a horizontal row are attached, in order of color, to a bridle. This is then positioned alongside the loom. The lashes are of course in the same color order as the shuttles on the loom. The weaver does not have to watch a design as he weaves. Everything is programmed: the drawboy pulls the lashes in order; the weaver throws the shuttles in order. Extensive patterns required three or four sets of these lashes and bridles to be attached to the loom in turn. (Reproduced from The Paisley Shawl *by Matthew Blair)*

With the Jacquard, the patterns were punched into cards according to the calculations of specialists. The weaver no longer even programmed the loom by tying and threading for a specific pattern. The cards, laced in order, held the pattern. When these laced cards were affixed in a Jacquard, the loom could produce the pattern. The Jacquard cards had some of the wonder and mystery of a player piano: a piano holds a musical composition within an irregular distribution of punched holes. The Jacquard cards held Paisley patterns.

Sometimes a single Jacquard attachment was used on a loom; sometimes several were used simultaneously, each with its own set of cards. Borders were frequently operated by one Jacquard while the remainder of the shawl was operated by one or two others. Sometimes the old drawloom mechanism and the Jacquard were used together to achieve a single piece of complex weaving.

With the talims and the Jacquard cards, patterns could be woven by weavers who had never seen the drawing or painting. Visual patterns could be read and spoken, transmitted by words and symbols. How contemporary the idea seems, akin to twentieth century artists' concern with being able to produce paintings by following instructions given over a telephone.

By conceiving of weaving not as linear elements running horizontally and vertically as the weaver sees them when he designs at his loom, but as points in a grid, each square representing a crossing of warp and weft, designers were able to plan textiles quite different in appearance from those that result from designing on the loom or from following a freely-drawn cartoon.

With patterns worked out with pencils, compasses, rulers and erasers on graph paper, designers were able to explore effects denied to direct designers. For example, interlaced patterns, the intellectual exercises of Moresque art and Irish illuminations, could be woven. Coptic weavers had revelled in similar effects in their tapestries. Sculptors had done the impossible by rendering them in stone and wood. Now such designs of even greater complexity could be woven over entire huge textiles.

(Opposite) Page from a book of ribbons, mostly English, 1860–65. The Jacquard was used for intricately-patterned ribbons, many including the Paisley motive. Just as the nineteenth century delighted in the elaborate shawl patterns that the Jacquards made possible, it found satisfaction in fine line engravings rendered in silk threads. Like the shawls, these illustrative ribbons required very many threads in warp and weft, and very many cards.
(Crown copyright: Victoria & Albert Museum)

Smooth curves required many graph paper squares. A point paper design might fill an entire room. Many squares meant that many fine threads had to be woven. Fine yarns demanded the mechanical looms that, as extensions of the hand, made possible what the hand, unassisted, could do only theoretically.

Certain patterning came naturally to the early mechanical drawlooms: precise repetition of rather small, regularly spaced, motives and larger motives with bilateral symmetry. Patterns were comber repeats and point repeats. Comber repeats gave relatively small motives repeated side by side. Point repeats gave motives twice as wide, with bilateral symmetry. The same loom could be threaded for either kind or for a combination of both.

(Right) Woven Paisley silk shawl. The warps were threaded through the drawloom in groups. This threading made large patterns possible with the early drawlooms, but it also made patterns composed of small squares. (Crown copyright: Victoria & Albert Museum)

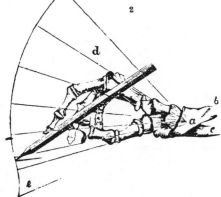

(Left) Designers drew curvilinear foliage according to rules based on geometric principles. Students learned to draw freehand according to rules and to work with the compass to draw elipses and curves. (From Guide for Drawing the Acanthus *by I. Page)*

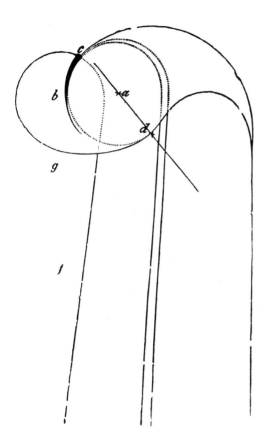

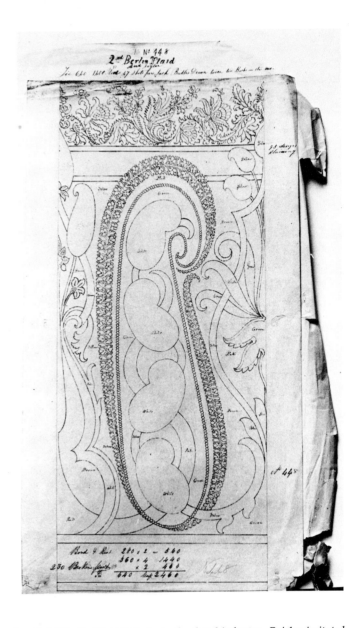

Art schools taught students to draw in the florid ornamental style, useful not only for textile designers but for ornamental workers in every department of the fine arts. The curves were developed according to geometric principles. In praising a handbook of rules and practice, a reviewer says, ". . . our English ornamental designers are nearly all of them slavish copyists, and scarcely dream of thinking for themselves, while they can beg, borrow, or steal from the wits of France." (From Guide for Drawing the Acanthus by I. Page)

Drafted design for a Paisley shawl, called "Berlin Plaid." Early in the shawl industry, Paisley imitated designs from Kashmir. As soon as shawls arrived from the East, their designs were copied by agents in London who quickly sent drawings to Paisley. In later years, Paisley looked to France for shawl designs. Pattern books from Paris set the styles after 1840; French designs were thought to be the best. While Paisley manufacturers ruthlessly copied or traced the successful designs from their various competitors, they also bought many French designs. These were purchased as renderings in full color on oiled paper that allowed designs to be traced from the originals. Over the years, Paisley developed its own designers who created original shawl designs. This "Berlin Plaid" is ready to be transferred to graph paper. (Collection: Paisley Museum and Art Galleries)

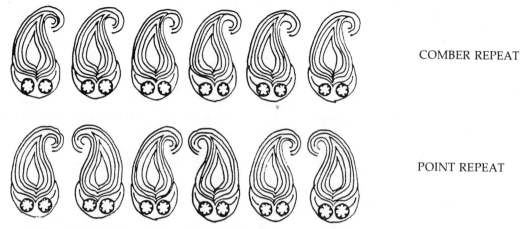

COMBER REPEAT

POINT REPEAT

These are the two basic repeats possible on a drawloom. The comber repeats the motive identically; the point repeats by alternating the directions of the motives. In this example, the comber shows six identical motives, while the point shows what can be regarded as three identical motives—each twice as large as a single comber motive. Point repeats were used to increase the apparent size of motives without increasing the size of the draw mechanism.

Skilled designers used these drawloom repeats to achieve infinite varieties of patterns. Yet designers felt frustrated by the limitations. Improvements kept being made for weaving larger motives. The Jacquard was a wonderful breakthrough. With it a motive could extend from selvage to selvage without a repeat and without bilateral symmetry. The formalizing central axis was eliminated, even in very wide textiles. (As long as the earlier drawloom textiles such as silk brocades were very narrow, a width of cloth could often avoid the appearance of strict symmetry in favor of the more sprawling and casual arrangements that were desired. But textiles as wide as shawls required symmetry until the Jacquard.) Patterns could spread in extravagant curves and infinite elaborations of details, limited only by the dimensions of the cloth and the willingness of a worker to punch many cards by the tedious methods then current.

Myriad flowers and branches were forced to adapt their configurations to the mechanical curves of the drawing board. Somehow the gears, cams, wheels, the multitude of incomprehensible parts of the new machinery, all fitting together, seem reflected in the Paisley shawls designed to please the fashionable woman while pleasing also the new technicians. Paisleys became the clearest and the most confident declarations of the mechanical. They spoke of the new era of abundance of fancy textiles and liberation from the fiber chores that had grown so heavy. Abundance and liberation were achieved through the machine. Small wonder that Paisley shawls were so admired and adored. They were unprecedented in the textile arts—the triumph of the mechanical loom that Europe embraced.

Today the shawls are difficult to approach without bias. Certainly they say "Victorian" so unmistakably that they share all the judgments against that era. It is undeniable that Paisley patterns were reworked so frequently that they were carried to extravagant extremes, extravagant distortions. And that shawls varied in quality and in the beauty of color and pattern. Yet, as we reassess the art of the nineteenth century and envy its exuberance and confidence, we recognize that even those Paisleys guilty of what are considered Victorian lapses in taste show qualities not so reprehensible.

Perhaps foremost among these, providing positive aesthetic satisfaction, is a clearly expressed technological orientation. Fiber has been controlled, ordered, harnessed to man's bidding. Instead of showing the mark of the hand, the textiles show the mark of the machine. Fiber has been worked into the finest, most perfect yarns manipulated beyond easy comprehension. Patterns repeat with precision—the repetition suggests the mechanical beat of the loom. The verticals and horizontals of warp and weft are approached as a sort of ruled graph paper for working out geometric designs. Compass lines are

(Right) Woven silk shawl, Norwich, third quarter nineteenth century. The mechanical scrolls suggest simultaneously architectural drafting tools and Celtic patterns, while the insistent mechanical scallops recall the contemporary machine lace. The large end panel is created by four point repeats. (Crown copyright: Victoria & Albert Museum)

British woven shawl, 1826–27. This shawl varies the direction of the motives by using a point repeat. The small borders have been added as separate pieces. (Crown copyright: Victoria & Albert Museum)

Cashmere woven shawl, nineteenth century. This handsome textile shows how far the Cashmere shawls went to satisfy the European market. Designs appropriate to Jacquard weaving were rendered, miraculously, as twill-tapestry. (The Metropolitan Museum of Art, Gift of Mrs. Henry Ivison Parsons, 1925)

Printed Paisley-type shawl, French, first half nineteenth century. The shawl is not an imitation of a woven shawl although the printed motives relate to the woven grid. (The Metropolitan Museum of Art, Gift of Mrs. David Dows, 1924)

accurately transcribed into weaving—a remarkable and pleasurable feat. The mechanical, rational look associates Paisleys, even those that are most densely embellished, with Byzantine silks and certain stark weavings from Northern Europe, not by imitating images or compositions (the aspects of other art that Paisleys so freely borrow), but by expressing the mechanical nature of the loom and the excitement and challenge of the grid of woven structure.

Nowadays the weavings of ancient Peru are greatly admired; they fit today's concepts of handweaving. Achieved by laborious hand methods on primitive looms, they are the antithesis of today's powerweaving. We respond to them with wonder and disbelief, sensing in them values we have lost.

By contrast the Victorian Paisleys are modern. They exemplify Europe's surge toward the technological. Although handwoven, they appear as mechanical as everything in our society; they are celebrations of the machine. As they depart farther and farther from the Asian models to become European textiles, they begin to look as though they had been woven on today's powerlooms. Finally, it is not their "Victorianism" that interferes with our full appreciation, but rather their modernism. They seem to us less remarkable than they are.

WEAVE WITH BACK OF CLOTH FACING WEAVER.

USING A 4-HARNESS LOOM, THREAD THE WARP
IN THE REGULAR TWILL THREADING.

 THREADING

 TREADLING

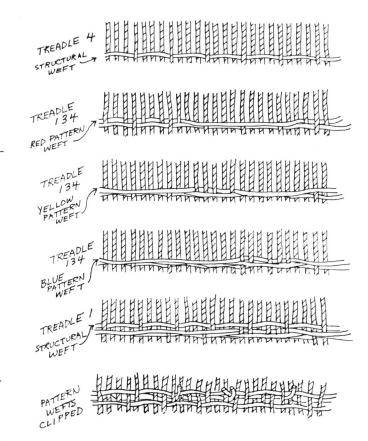

TREADLE 4 STRUCTURAL WEFT

TREADLE 134 RED PATTERN WEFT

TREADLE 134 YELLOW PATTERN WEFT

TREADLE 134 BLUE PATTERN WEFT

TREADLE 1 STRUCTURAL WEFT

PATTERN WEFTS CLIPPED

TREADLE 4 - INSERT STRUCTURAL WEFT - BEAT

TREADLE 134 - INSERT PATTERN WEFT "A"
ALLOWING IT TO ENTER SHED
ONLY WHERE REQUIRED BY THE
PATTERN. OTHERWISE LET IT
FLOAT ON THE SURFACE. BEAT

TREADLE 134 - INSERT PATTERN WEFT "B" AS
REQUIRED. BEAT

TREADLE 134 - INSERT PATTERN WEFT "C" AS
REQUIRED. BEAT.

TREADLE 1 - INSERT STRUCTURAL WEFT - BEAT

TREADLE 124 - INSERT PATTERN WEFT "A", "B",
"C". - BEAT

TREADLE 2 - INSERT STRUCTURAL WEFT - BEAT

TREADLE 123 - INSERT PATTERN WEFT "A", "B",
"C". - BEAT

TREADLE 3 - INSERT STRUCTURAL WEFT - BEAT

TREADLE 234 - INSERT PATTERN WEFT "A", "B",
"C" - BEAT

REPEAT

CLIP FLOATS AFTER WEAVING IS OFF THE LOOM.

Theoretically a Paisley shawl could be woven on a 4-harness loom by using much hand manipulation in inserting the wefts to create the pattern. These instructions show how it might be done to give a semblance of Paisley patterning. Actually, the fineness of the yarns and the complexity of the designs—which characterize Paisleys—make the process not feasible except on a mechanical loom.

Text References

1.   J. Grassick, *The Paisley Shawl*, p. 15.
2.   Thomas W. Leavitt, "Fashion, Commerce and Technology in the Nineteenth Century: The Shawl Trade," *Textile History* Volume 3, p. 51.
3.   Victoria and Albert Museum, *Fifty Masterpieces of Textiles*, Plate 16.
4.   W. Born, "The Crinoline," *Ciba Review* No. 46, May 1943, p. 1676.
5.   *The Ladies Companion*, quoted in Christopher Denyer, "Golden Fleeces," *Ciba-Geigy Journal* No. 2/73, p. 30.
6.   Clinton G. Gilroy, *The Art of Weaving by Hand and by Power*, p. 54.
7.   Sir Walter Scott, *Rob Roy*, p. 267.
8.   David Gilmour, *Reminiscences of the Pen' Folk, Paisley Weavers of Other Days, etc.*, p. 28.
9.   Ibid. p. 10.
10.   Ibid. p. 14.
11.   Ibid. pp. 12 and 17.
12.   Mary McCarthy, *A Social Geography of Paisley*, p. 83.
13.   Duncan Bythell, *The Handloom Weavers*, p. 138.
14.   William Jolly, *John Duncan Weaver and Botanist*, p. 21, as quoted by Brenda Gaskin in her unpublished thesis, p. 223.
15.   J. C. Symons, *Arts and Artisans at Home and Abroad*, p. 147, as quoted by Brenda Gaskin in her unpublished thesis, p. 223.
16.   Whitworth Art Gallery, University of Manchester, Slide Set notes No. C6754 regarding William Morris.
17.   E. A. Posselt, *Technology of Textile Design*, p. 256.
18.   Luther Hooper, *The New Draw-loom*, p. 6.
19.   Webster's *New World Dictionary*, 1968.
20.   John Irwin, *The Kashmir Shawl*, p. 2.

Bibliography

Annan, Thomas. *Photographs of the Old Closes and Streets of Glasgow 1868/1877.* New York: Dover Publications, Inc., 1977.

Beaumont, Roberts. *The Finishing of Textile Fabrics.* London: Scott, Greenwood & Son, 1926.

Beer, Alice Baldwin. *Trade Goods, A Study of Indian Chintz.* Washington: Smithsonian Institution Press, 1970.

Blair, Matthew. *The Paisley Shawl and the Men who Produced It.* Paisley: Alexander Gardner, 1904.

Born, W., "The Crinoline," *Ciba Review,* Basle, No. 46 "Crinoline and Bustle," No. 46, May 1943.

Bremner, David. *The Industries of Scotland.* Edinburgh: Adam and Charles Black, 1869.

Buckley, Jerome Hamilton. *The Victorian Temper.* New York: Vintage Books, 1951.

Burnham, Harold B. *Handweaving in Pioneer Canada.* Toronto: Royal Ontario Museum, 1976.

Bythell, Duncan. *The Handloom Weavers.* Cambridge: University Press, 1969.

Cathcart, Florence B. "The Pros and Cons of Fly-Shuttle Weaving," *The Handicrafter,* November-December 1931.

Chattopadhyaya, Kamaladevi. *Carpets and Floor Coverings of India.* Bombay: Taraporevala, 1969.

Christie, Archibald H. *Pattern Design.* New York: Dover Publications, Inc., 1929, republished 1969.

Clabburn, Pamela. "Norwich Shawls." *Norfolk Museums Service Information Sheet,* Norfolk Museums Service, 1975.

Crystal Palace Exhibition, The. *Illustrated Catalogue, London 1851.* New York: Dover Publications, Inc., 1970.

124   Denyer, Christopher. "Golden Fleeces." *Ciba-Geigy Journal* No. 2/73 Summer.

Diderot, Denis. *Planches pour l'Encyclopédie, ou pour le Dictionnaire raisonné des sciences, des arts et des métiers (1765–76).*

Duncan, John. *Practical and Descriptive Essays on the Art of Weaving.* Glasgow, 1808.

English, W. *The Textile Industry.* London: Longmans , Green & Co., Ltd., 1969.

Evans, Joan. *Pattern, A Study of Ornament in Western Europe, Vol. II, From 1180 to 1900.* New York: DaCapo Press, Inc., 1931, reprinted 1976.

Faraday, Cornelia Bateman. *European and American Carpets and Rugs.* Grand Rapids: The Dean-Hicks Co., 1929.

Fox, Thomas W. *The Mechanism of Weaving.* London: MacMillan & Co., Ltd., 1911.

Gaskin, Brenda. *The Decline of the Hand-Loom Weaving Industry in Scotland during the Years 1815–1845.* Unpublished Ph.D. dissertation, Edinburgh University.

Gilmour, David. *Reminiscences of The Pen' Folk, Paisley Weavers of Other Days, Etc.* Paisley: Alex Gardner, 1889.

Gilroy, Clinton G. *The Art of Weaving by Hand and by Power.* London: Wiley & Putnam, 1845.

Grant, I. F. *The Economic History of Scotland.* London: Longmans, Green and Co., 1934.

Grassick, J. *The Paisley Shawl.* Grand Forks, North Dakota: Holt Printing Co., 1926.

Hamilton, Henry. *The Industrial Revolution in Scotland.* Oxford: The Clarendon Press, 1932.

Hindson, Alice. *Designer's Drawloom.* London: Faber and Faber Ltd., 1958.

Hobsbawm, E. J. *Industry and Empire.* Baltimore: Penguin Books, 1969.

Hooper, Luther. *The New Draw-loom.* London: Sir Isaac Pitman & Sons, Ltd., 1932.

——————— *Silk, Its Production and Manufacture.* London: Sir Isaac Pitman & Sons, Ltd., 1919.

Hunter, George Leland. *Decorative Textiles.* Philadelphia: Lippincott, 1918.

Hunter, Jim. "The Paisley Textile Industry, 1695–1830." *Costume, The Journal of the Costume Society,* No. 10, 1976.

Irwin, John. *The Kashmir Shawl.* London: Her Majesty's Stationery Office, 1973.

——————— *Shawls.* London: Her Majesty's Stationery Office, 1955.

Johnson, Samuel. *Journey to the Western Islands of Scotland.* Oxford: Oxford University Press, 1924, reprinted 1974.

Johnstone, Pauline. *Greek Island Embroidery.* London: Alec Tiranti, 1961.

Karpinski, Caroline. "Kashmir to Paisley." *The Metropolitan Museum of Art Bulletin,* November 1963.

Krishna, Rai Anand, and Krishna, Vijay. *Banaras Brocades.* New Delhi: Crafts Museum, 1966.

Leavitt, Thomas W. "Fashion, Commerce and Technology in the Nineteenth Century: The Shawl Trade." *Textile History,* Volume 3, 1972.

MacKinnon, James. *The Social and Industrial History of Scotland.* London: Longmans, Green and Co., 1921.

MacMillan, Susan L. *Greek Island Embroideries.* Boston: Museum of Fine Arts.

McCarthy, Mary. *A Social Geography of Paisley.* Paisley: Committee of Management, Paisley Public Library, 1969.

Meyer, Franz Sales. *A Handbook of Ornament.* New York: Architectural Book Publishing Co., Inc., 1892.

Mossman, Rachael G. "Design Techniques of Kashmir Handloom Textiles." *Bulletin of the Needle and Bobbin Club,* Vol. 50, Nos. 1 and 2, 1967.

Le Musée de L'Impression sur Etoffes de Mulhouse. *No. 761-4/1975 du Bulletin de la Société Industrielle de Mulhouse.* Mulhouse: L'Alsace, 1975.

Obenshain, Eliza Caroline (Calvert) [Eliza Calvert Hall]. *Book of Handwoven Coverlets.* Boston: Little, Brown & Co., 1912.

Olson, Eleanor. "The Textiles and Costumes of India: A Historical Review." Newark: Newark Museum Association, *The Museum,* Summer/Fall 1965.

Özbel, Kenan. *El Sanatlari,* Pamphlet XIII Woven Shawls, Görün Sallari. Ankara: C.H.P. Halkevleri Bürosu, 1949.

Page, I. *Guide for Drawing the Acanthus and Every Description of Ornamental Foliage.* London: Bernard Quaritch, reprinted 1886.

Paisley Museum and Art Galleries. *Old Paisley in Pictures, Parts 1 and 2.* Paisley: Museum and Art Galleries, 1970.

Paisley Shawls: A Chapter of the Industrial Revolution. Paisley: Ramshorn Press.

Perleberg, Hans Carl. *Persian Textiles, Second Series.* Jersey City: H. C. Perleberg, 1919.

Piton, Camille. *Le Costume Civil en France du XIIIe au XIXe Siécle.* Paris: E. Flammarion, 1913.

Posselt, E. A. *Technology of Textile Design.* London: Sampson Low, Marston & Co., Ltd., 189-

Rock, C. H. *Paisley Shawls, A Chapter of the Industrial Revolution.* Paisley: Museum and Art Galleries, 1966.

Rodier, Paul. *The Romance of French Weaving.* New York: Tudor Publishing Co., 1936.

126   Rothstein, Natalie. *Spitalfields Silks.* London: Her Majesty's Stationery Office, 1975.

Scott, Sir Walter. *Rob Roy.* London: Thomas Nelson and Sons, 1901.

Simonson, Lee. "Fashion and Democracy." *The Metropolitan Museum of Art Bulletin,* November 1944.

Slaven, Anthony. *The Development of the West of Scotland 1750–1960.* London: Routledge & Kegan Paul, 1975.

Sobolev, N. *A History of Textile Design.* Translated by Eugenia Tolmachoff. Moscow-Leningrad 1934.

Swain, Margaret H. *The Flowerers.* London: W. & R. Chambers, Ltd., 1955.

——————— *Historical Needlework.* London: Barrie & Jenkins, 1970.

Tuchscherer, Jean-Michel. *The Fabrics of Mulhouse and Alsace.* Leigh-on-Sea: F. Lewis, Publishers, Ltd.

Twiss, Travers. *Two Lectures on Machinery.* Delivered before the University of Oxford in 1844. Shannon: Irish University Press, 1972.

Varnedoe, Kirk. "The Grand Party that was the Second Empire." *Art News,* December 1978.

Victoria and Albert Museum. *Fifty Masterpieces of Textiles.* London: Her Majesty's Stationery Office, 1951, reprinted 1958.

West Surrey College of Art and Design. Catalog of Exhibition "The Art of the Shawls." Autumn 1977.

Whyte, Dorothy. "Edinburgh Shawls and their Makers." *Costume, The Journal of the Costume Society,* No. 10, 1976.

Wyatt, M. Digby. *Industrial Arts of the 19th Century.* London: Day and Son, 1853.

Yale University Art Gallery. *The Kashmir Shawl.* New Haven: Meriden Gravure Company, 1975.

Index

Page numbers in italics indicate illustrations.